POPE BENEDICT XVI

The Conscience of Our Age

POPE BENEDICT XVI

The Conscience of Our Age

A Theological Portrait

by

D. Vincent Twomey, S.V.D.

IGNATIUS PRESS   SAN FRANCISCO

Sermon by Pope Benedict XVI
Castel Gandolfo, September 4, 2005
© Libreria Editrice Vaticana
English translation © by Martin Henry
All rights reserved
Used with permission

Cover photograph of Pope Benedict XVI
by Stefano Spaziani

Cover design by Roxanne Mei Lum

© 2007 by Ignatius Press, San Francisco
All rights reserved
ISBN 978-1-58617-170-4
Library of Congress Control Number 2006924093
Printed in the United States of America ⊗

The least power of love is already greater than the greatest power of destruction.

—Salt of the Earth

And as a result [of living through the Nazi period], I learned to have a certain reserve with regard to the reigning ideologies.

—Interview, 1993

My real program of governance is not to do my own will, not to pursue my own ideas, but to listen, together with the whole Church, to the word and the will of the Lord, to be guided by him, so that he himself will lead the Church at this hour of our history.

—Homily at the Inauguration Mass on April 24, 2005

CONTENTS

INTRODUCTION

THE COURAGE TO BE IMPERFECT

Walking the streets of Rome the day before Pope Benedict XVI's Inauguration Mass,[1] I was confronted by a strange
and rather unsettling sight: the familiar face of my former
teacher in hundreds of posters everywhere. They were on
billboards and in street stalls among miniature statues of
Michelangelo's *Pietà* and *David*, or they were stuck in-
congruously between bottles of grappa in a café. I had
arrived in Rome that Saturday morning and was one of
the vast crowd walking toward the magnificent piazza in
front of Saint Peter's Basilica, still somewhat numbed by
shock that the man whom I had long revered as *Doktorvater* had just been elected pope, the new successor of

[1] The booklet with the text of the Mass was entitled: *Inauguration of the
Petrine Ministry of the Bishop of Rome*. It seems to be of no small significance
that neither the term *Summus Pontifex* nor any related title is mentioned in
the liturgical booklet. Like the replacement of the papal tiara, or triple crown,
with a simple bishop's miter in the Pope's coat of arms (albeit with traces of
the tiara in the miter), this preferred title (*the Petrine Ministry of the Bishop of
Rome*) probably signifies a change of emphasis for the papacy, although one
that is rooted in the most ancient traditions of the Church universal, in particular, that of the pre-Constantinian era. It might well augur a new era in
ecumenical relations, especially with the Orthodox and Oriental Churches
no longer in communion with the Bishop of Rome.

Saint Peter. Joseph Ratzinger himself has written extensively on the nature of the office of the pope,[2] and at least
three of his doctoral students[3] have devoted their research
to the origins and nature of the primacy of the Bishop of
Rome in the universal Church, which is one of the chief
stumbling blocks for separated Christians, in fact the only
really substantial obstacle to union with the Orthodox
Churches.

It was only in the course of the various celebrations mark-
ing his inauguration as successor of Saint Peter that I slowly
came to terms with the transformation of my former teacher,
an eminent but essentially humble German professor, into
the Universal Pastor of the Church, now the focus of the
world's attention, thanks in no small way to the modern
mass media. The somewhat retiring academic I had once
known had become an exuberant pastor, responding with
gestures we his former students had never seen before, such
as waving hands and kissing babies.

While I was in Rome, the main topic of conversation
was the person of the new Pope. Everyone wanted to know:
What kind of a person is he? Those who had only known

---

[2] See, for example, Karl Rahner and Joseph Ratzinger, *Episkopat und Pri-
mat,* Quaestiones Disputatae 11 (Freiburg im Breisgau: Herder, 1961); J. Ratzinger, *Das neue Volk Gottes: Entwürfe zur Ekklesiologie* (Düsseldorf: Patmos,
1969); "Papal Primacy and the Unity of the People of God", in *Church,
Ecumenism and Politics: New Essays in Ecclesiology* [= *CEP*], trans. Robert Nowell (Slough: Saint Paul; New York: Crossroad, 1988), pp. 29–45; *Called to
Communion: Understanding the Church Today,* trans. Adrian Walker (San Francisco: Ignatius Press, 1996), especially chap. 2, pp. 47–74.

[3] M. Trimpe, *Macht aus Gehorsam: Grundmotive der Theologie des päpstlichen
Primates im Denken Reginald Poles (1500–1558)* (dissertation, Regensburg, 1981);
Stephan Otto Horn, *Petrou Kathedra: Der Bischof von Rom und die Synoden von
Ephesus und Chalcedon* (Paderborn: Verlag Bonifatius-Druckerei, 1982); Vin-
cent Twomey, *Apostolikos Thronos: The Primacy of Rome as Reflected in the Church
History of Eusebius and the Historico-Apologetic Writings of Saint Athanasius the
Great* (Münster: Aschendorff, 1982).

the new Pope as the Cardinal Prefect of the Congregation for the Doctrine of the Faith had a decidedly negative image, one largely created not only by a largely hostile media but also by the nature of his office as Cardinal Prefect responsible for the integrity of the faith.[4] That image did not match the reality they now saw on their TV screens, and so they asked: "What is he really like?" His former grim image was strikingly at variance with the smiling new Pope, who had evidently captured the hearts of the Romans and who was already causing journalists from around the world to question their own creation.

When we, his former students, some of whom had known him for forty-five years, got together in private, we allowed ourselves the luxury of fond—and not so fond—reminiscences. Over lunches that lasted well into the afternoon, we recalled the halcyon days when we were his postgraduate or postdoctoral students. The atmosphere in Rome was comparable to that of a wedding banquet: we tried to accustom ourselves—not without an occasional tear and much laughter—to the sudden change of our much beloved teacher into the Holy Father, who was now exciting the world as he had once inspired his students in Regensburg. In truth, we could hardly contain our joy or adequately express our surprise at the fact that our former teacher had become the successor of Saint Peter as Bishop of Rome, whose main task would be to nourish the faith and strengthen the brethren, his fellow bishops and all

---

[4] The effect of his negative image is well illustrated by the reaction of an old friend, an S.Sp.S. Sister, to whom I had given *To Look on Christ*, one of Ratzinger's spiritual works, as a present quite some time ago. She did not even bother to open the book. During Advent one year, she got the courage to take it off the shelf—only to be quite overwhelmed by the richness of his reflections. She has since reread the book so often that it has come apart!

fellow Christians, in our common mission and responsibility to bring Christ to mankind and lead mankind to Christ.

The world at last, we felt, had the opportunity to encounter the charming personality, intellectual brilliance, and pastoral heart of the man we his former students knew so well. This encounter was made possible by journalists, the very people, paradoxically, who had been largely responsible for his negative image as "Grand Inquisitor", *Panzerkardinal* (the iron-clad cardinal), and "enforcer of the faith" (John L. Allen, Jr.). Incidentally, at an audience of some five thousand journalists and their relatives the day before his induction, Benedict XVI thanked them for making it possible for the world to participate in the recent death of the Pope and the election of a successor, often at great personal cost to themselves and their families. It was the first time they had been thanked by a pope, one hardened journalist told me, and they were deeply moved.

We, his former students, recalled the days when he was a professor in Bonn, Münster, Tübingen, and, especially, Regensburg. We were displeased by the recent attempt to blacken his image by distorting the truth about his youth at a time when Germany was under the total control of Hitler. (He and his family were intensely anti-Nazi.) [5] And we speculated about the future, about what he might do, in the light of what we knew of his own personality and, more importantly, of his great mind and extraordinary memory.

Pope Benedict XVI will teach the world not only by what he says but also by example. The simple dignity of the Requiem for Pope John Paul II and the sheer beauty of his own Inauguration Mass gave those present a touch of heaven on earth—and entranced those who followed it on television. As I remarked to a Dublin diocesan priest, now

---

[5] I will deal with this topic below in chap. 6.

studying liturgy in Rome, who sat near me at the Mass: Benedict XVI was giving the world his first lesson in liturgy. He has written extensively on liturgy, but his writings have generally been ignored—even kept off the shelves of at least one institute set up for the study of liturgy, as I happen to know. Now, it is hoped, people will finally read him.

This, I suspect, will be his teaching method—first to win the hearts of people, who will then read for themselves what he has written on a particular topic. He has written on almost every theological subject touching on the faith, morality, and Church and State. The latest bibliography of his publications (up to 2002) covers some seventy-nine pages.[6] Many more publications have appeared since then—the latest a few weeks after his election as Pope Benedict XVI,[7] for, as few people realize, he continued to publish as a private theologian while Prefect of the Congregation for the Doctrine of the Faith.

What is the secret of Ratzinger's quiet, dignified behavior, as seen during the world-shaking events of Pope John Paul II's

---

[6] Joseph Ratzinger, *Pilgrim Fellowship of Faith: The Church as Communion*, a collection of articles published as a book by his former doctoral and post-doctoral students on the occasion of his seventy fifth birthday and edited by Stephan Otto Horn and Vinzenz Pfnür (San Francisco: Ignatius Press, 2005); the bibliography is on pp. 299–379. For the most complete *annotated* bibliography up to 1986, see that compiled by Helmut Höfl in *Weisheit Gottes— Weisheit der Welt*, vol. 2, *Festschrift für Kardinal Ratzinger zum 60. Geburtstag*, ed. Walter Baier et al. (St. Ottilien: EOS Verlag, 1986), pp. 1*–77*. For the period from 1986 to 1997, see the bibliography of original publications (including secondary literature on his theology) compiled by Helmut Moll and *thematically arranged in Joseph Kardinal Ratzinger: Von Wiederauffinden der Mitte: Grundorientierung; Texte aus vier Jahrzehnten*, ed. Stephan Otto Horn, S.D.S., et al. (Freiburg im Breisgau: Herder, 1997; 2nd printing 1998), pp. 291–315.

[7] Joseph Ratzinger, *L'Europa di Benedetto nella crisi delle culture*. Introduzione Marcello Pera (Siena: Edizioni Cantagalli, 2005); English trans.: *The Europe of Benedict in the Crisis of Cultures*, trans. Brian McNeil, C.R.V. (San Francisco: Ignatius Press, 2006).

death and the conclave that elected him successor? How could he be so relaxed and smiling precisely at the moment he accepted his election to responsibilities that would overwhelm most mortals? Let me answer by recalling two anecdotes.

While at Tübingen, one student asked another to identify the difference between Professor Ratzinger and another equally famous theologian. The reply was: Ratzinger also finds time to play the piano. He is as open to beauty as he is to truth. He lives outside himself. He is not preoccupied with his own self. Put simply, he does not take himself too seriously.

The other anecdote is personal. Once he asked me gently about the progress of my thesis. It was about time, as I had been working on it for some seven years. I told him that I thought there was still some work to be done. He turned to me with those piercing but kindly eyes, saying with a smile: "Nur Mut zur Lücke" (Have the courage to leave some gaps). In other words, be courageous enough to be imperfect.

On reflection, this is one of the keys to Ratzinger's character (and also to his theology, in particular his theology of politics): his acceptance that everything we do is imperfect, that all knowledge is limited, no matter how brilliant or well read one may be. It never bothered him that in a course of lectures he rarely covered the actual content of the course. His most famous book, *Introduction to Christianity*, is incomplete.[8] Ratzinger knows in his heart and soul that God alone

---

[8] Joseph Ratzinger, *Introduction to Christianity* [= *IC*], trans. J. R. Foster (London: Burns and Oates, 1969). The book was intended to be a commentary on the Creed, but in fact the third article (on the Holy Spirit) is but a fragment. The genesis of this, perhaps the most well known of all his writings, is interesting. In the preface to the first edition (1968), he wrote: "The book arose out of lectures which I gave at Tübingen in the summer term of 1967 for students of all faculties." The lectures were tape-recorded by one of his *Assistenten*, Doctor Peter Kuhn, who made a transcript of the tape. He gave the transcript to Professor Ratzinger to edit and insert the footnotes, which was done during the summer vacation. A second edition with a new

is perfect and that all human attempts at perfection (such as political utopias) end in disaster.

The only perfection open to us is that advocated by Jesus in the Gospel: "You, therefore, must be perfect, as your heavenly Father is perfect" (Mt 5:48), he who "makes his sun rise on the evil and on the good, and sends rain on the just and on the unjust" (Mt 5:45). Love of God and love of neighbor: that is the secret of Pope Benedict XVI, and that will be the core of his universal teaching.[9]

*   *   *

Chapters 1, 3, 4, and 5 are revised versions of an article, "La coscienza e l'uomo", that was my contribution to the Festschrift in honor of Joseph Cardinal Ratzinger's seventieth birthday.[10] Most of chapter 2 and the end of chapter 4 were originally published in the *Claremont Review of Books* (Fall 2005) under the title "The Mind of Benedict XVI" and are reproduced here with permission.[11] The above introduction is a slightly revised version of an article, "The Courage to Be Imperfect", first published in *The Word*, June 2005. Chapter 7 originally appeared as an article in the *Irish*

---

preface was published in German in 2000, with an English translation in 2004 (San Francisco: Ignatius Press).

[9] This was written in May 2005. My prognostication has been confirmed, not only by the first encyclical from the pen of Pope Benedict XVI, *Deus Caritas Est*, which has the interaction of divine and human loves as its subject matter, but also by many of his addresses and messages, such as his Address to the Roman Curia, December 22, 2005.

[10] *Alla scuola della Verità: I settanta anni di Joseph Ratzinger*, ed. Josef Clemens and Antonio Tarzia (Cinisello Balsamo [Milan]: San Paolo, 1997), pp. 111–45.

[11] The text has been significantly revised as the introduction to *The Essential Benedict XVI: His Central Writings and speeches*, ed. John F. Thornton and Susan B. Varenne (San Francisco: HarperSanFrancisco, 2007), pp. xvii–xxxviii.

Independent, April 21, 2005. Apart from the last, all have been revised for this publication.

I am most grateful to Lisa Tierney, Father Stephan O. Horn, S.D.S., and Msgr. Joseph Murphy for reading earlier drafts of the manuscript with such care and attention and for their invaluable corrections, comments, and suggestions, as also Brother Paul Hurley, S.V.D., who read the penultimate version, and Henrich Barlage, S.V.D., Lore Bartholomäus, Martin Trimpe, and Peter Bornhausen, who made invaluable contributions (and corrections) to the final version. A special word of thanks to Martin Henry for his excellent translation of the Pope's sermon (in the appendix). I accept full responsibility for the infelicities or errors that remain. My special thanks are due to Father Joseph Fessio, S.J., and the staff at Ignatius Press for accepting the manuscript and the care they took in its production. I should like to single out Anne Nash, who copy edited the manuscript with great care and precision. My final thanks are due to the present successor of Saint Peter, who directed my doctoral research. His writings and personal example have been, and are, a continual source of inspiration. His gracious permission to publish the sermon he preached (without a note) at the first meeting of his former doctoral and postdoctoral students, held in Castel Gandolfo, September 3, 2005, is but a token of his encouragement and friendship over the past thirty-five years. In gratitude, this book is dedicated to my one-time *Doktorvater*, now our Holy Father, Pope Benedict XVI.

Chapter One

THE CONSCIENCE OF THE TEACHER

Germany was still in turmoil, not least the German universities, when I arrived in Münster, Westphalia, to begin my postgraduate studies. It was two years after the student revolt of 1968, the year that, among other epoch-making events (such as the bloody end to the "Prague Spring" in Czechoslovakia and the beginning of the "Troubles" in Northern Ireland), saw the publication of *Humanae Vitae*, which almost split the Church in two. The student revolt heralded a left-wing swing in politics and quickly degenerated into terrorism, a phenomenon that Joseph Ratzinger would later diagnose as a symptom of an underlying illness in society, an illness whose roots were intellectual and ultimately theological.[1] Pope Paul VI's encyclical on birth control was the watershed in the postconciliar period that polarized the Church into those, on the one hand, who, claiming to follow "the spirit of Vatican II", rejected the

[1] *Turning Point for Europe? The Church in the Modern World—Assessment and Forecast* [= *TPE*], trans. Brian McNeil, C.R.V. (San Francisco: Ignatius Press, 1994), pp. 21–24, 43–46. According to Ratzinger, the 1968 uprisings in Germany had their origin in the theology faculties, where partisanship for a better world replaced the confessional dimension. See his *CEP* 156.

encyclical and those, on the other hand, who looked with skepticism at the changes brought about in the name of renewal, appealed to tradition, and accepted the Pope's teaching.

The crisis caused by the publication of *Humanae Vitae* affected moral theology in the first place but also dogmatic theology, indeed, theology as a whole. What was at stake was the nature of the Church's teaching office and, thus, tradition, the perception of which had radically changed in the aftermath of the Council. It soon became clear that the crisis was not simply an internal affair of the Church. It reflected nothing less than the crisis of Western civilization itself caused by the threefold rejection of moral objectivity, tradition, and a common human nature. The West German Bishops' Conference published their somewhat ambiguous response to *Humanae Vitae* in the *Königsteiner Erklärung*:[2] They accepted the papal teaching, but at the same time they encouraged people "to follow their own conscience", which was understood to mean acting, if one thought it

---

[2] Königstein in Taunus was the place where the West German Bishops' Conference, under the chairmanship of Archbishop Julius Cardinal Döpfner of Munich, met on August 29 and 30, 1968, to discuss the encyclical *Humanae Vitae*. They issued a declaration (*Erklärung*—in fact, they issued two, a shorter and a longer one) affirming the Pope's teaching. However, they added that "a responsible decision made in conscience must be respected by all", even, as many assumed, if it means that a Catholic might thereby deviate from an ecclesiastic decision that falls outside the scope of infallibility, which they claimed was the case with *Humanae Vitae* (see John Horgan, ed., *Humanae Vitae and the Bishops: The Encyclical and the Statements of the National Hierarchies* [Shannon: Irish University Press, 1972], p. 304). The East German bishops met in East Berlin, then the capital of the DDR (German Democratic Republic), under the presidency of Bishop Alfred Cardinal Bengsch of Berlin, and issued a totally positive declaration on September 10 (12), 1968, embracing the teaching without equivocation (see Horgan, *Humanae Vitae and the Bishops*, pp. 100–111).

right, in contradiction to the traditional teaching confirmed by Pope Paul VI. By papering over the cracks, the bishops may have kept the Church in West Germany together, but the cracks were fissures in the rock on which the Church is built.

Ratzinger would later devote considerable attention not only to the questions of authority and tradition, and the underlying ecclesiology, but also to the more fundamental question concerning the nature of moral theology within the wider context of the crisis of Western civilization.[3] The widespread rejection of *Humanae Vitae* by theologians and the compromise of the German bishops at Königstein found their justification in the new magic word that soon became identified with the heritage of the Council: *conscience*.

Conscience is a theme that Ratzinger would in later years take up and develop in particular. However, already in 1972, he had sketched the main contours of his subsequent reflections on conscience in a talk he gave to the Reinhold Schneider Gesellschaft.[4] His later responsibilities as Prefect of the Congregation for the Doctrine of the Faith made him confront issues in moral theology and politics, which allowed him to develop insights he had gleaned in his earlier dogmatic and, in particular, fundamental

---

[3] Interestingly, Ratzinger has, to the best of my knowledge, not commented expressly on the subject of the encyclical *Humanae Vitae*, published in 1968, even in his evaluation of the Second Vatican Council and its aftermath (see Joseph Ratzinger, *Principles of Catholic Theology: Building Stones for a Fundamental Theology* [= *PCT*], translated by Sister Mary Francis McCarthy, S.N.D. [San Francisco: Ignatius Press, 1987], pp. 367–93), when one might justifiably have expected a reference to that watershed in the postconciliar period. For his perceptive views on contraception see *SE* 200–203.

[4] Cf. *Internationale katholische Zeitschrift Communio* 1 (1972): 432–42; also in *Reinhold-Schneider-Gesellschaft e. V.*, Heft 4 (July 1972): 13–19; reprinted in *CEP* 165–80.

theological writings. Conscience, it seems to me, might well be a key concept to understanding both the personality of the man and his theology. More accurately it is the link between both. In this, and in the succeeding chapters, I will simply try to indicate briefly how this link can be understood and, at the same time, to outline Ratzinger's own understanding of conscience by sketching the role it plays in his teaching and theology. I will then examine his theology of conscience, the seeds of which were sown at the very beginning of his theological studies, when he first encountered the writings of John Henry Newman, thanks to the fact that his prefect in the seminary, Alfred Läpple, was working on a doctoral thesis devoted to Newman's understanding of conscience.[5]

Since theology, at least for Ratzinger, is not simply a scholarly exercise but a personal search for truth—"theology is a spiritual science",[6] he wrote, involving the theologian's own subjective relationship with God and with the friends of

[5] See Cardinal Joseph Ratzinger, "Newman Belongs to the Great Teachers of the Church: Introductory Words for the Third Day of the Newman Symposium in Rome [28 April 1990]", in Peter Jennings, ed., *Benedict XVI and Cardinal Newman* (Oxford: Family Publications, 2005), pp. 33–35 (here 33). See also Alfred Läpple, *Bendedikt XVI. und seine Wurzlen: Was den Studenten Joseph Ratzinger prägte* (Augsburg: St. Ulrich Verlag, 2006), pp. 58–63, which appeared after I had completed this book, as well as *Milestones: Memoirs 1927–1977* [=*MM*], trans. Erasmo Leiva-Merikakis (San Francisco: Ignatius Press, 1998), p. 43.

[6] See *PCT* 321. Commenting on this mediaeval understanding of theology, Ratzinger draws attention to the fact that, despite the fact that Abélard moved theology out of the monastery into the neutrality of academe, the following centuries never lost sight of the need for the requisite spiritual context for the study of theology. "It seems to me that it was only after World War II and completely only after Vatican Council II that we came to think that theology, like any exotic subject, can be studied from a purely academic perspective from which one acquires knowledge that can be useful in life" (322).

God—I may be excused for using my own experience as a starting point. This brings me back to Münster, Westphalia, in 1970, when I first came to Germany with the oil of ordination still wet on my hands and excitement in my heart at the opportunity of studying for a doctorate at a German university.

1. The university seminar

At Münster, I first sat at the feet of Professor Karl Rahner, then at the zenith of his fame, to hear him lecture on Christology and attend his higher seminar on the same subject. This was nothing if not ambitious, since my facility in German at the time fell somewhat short of the challenge posed by the Rahnerian use of the language. He was held in awe by everyone, an awe that, for some of us in the seminar, turned slowly to frustration. During the seminar, while a student read a paper, Professor Rahner would prowl up and down on one side of the packed room, seemingly impatient until the student's essay was over and he could begin. The rest of the seminar was a monologue, despite all our efforts to engage him in some kind of discussion. At the end of the semester I moved to Regensburg.

My first and most abiding memory of Ratzinger is of the way in which he conducted his seminars and his doctoral colloquium in Regensburg. Discussion reigned supreme. He had an ability to promote debate and encourage nervous beginners that has remained the model for my own teaching. He listened—carefully and shrewdly, indeed, but above all patiently—and remembered all the salient points raised in the discussion, which he allowed to run its course with the least possible interruption on his part. When it seemed apt, Ratzinger would finally intervene in an attempt to discern the main lines of the previous argument, develop them further, and show their theological implications, before going on to raise related questions. He would stop the session when the allotted time was up, often leaving some pertinent issue to be resolved until a later session, if at all, since many issues could not be decided in that forum. The ease and calm with which the various questions were treated, the patient attention to objections and difficulties, and the ability to allow issues to remain unresolved promoted further discussion in small groups after the seminar session—or encouraged us to return to the library for further research. In a word, the discussions he conducted were intellectually stimulating.

The way he handled these sessions also reveals Ratzinger the theologian, one who is continually searching for the truth, attentive to all objections, whether historical or contemporary, aware of human limitations, and open to insight or instruction from any source, even the opinions of a young student. I marveled at the way he could take up a point poorly expressed by some nervous beginner and rephrase it in his own words to the amazement of the student, who recognized what he had wanted to say now being expressed with a clarity and in language to which he could only at best aspire. It did not matter that the professor would then go on to show why such an opinion was untenable: one's thesis had been taken seriously, and one had good reasons to think again about one's opinion.

That capacity to create a space for a free and frank exchange of views was not simply a natural talent. It was rooted in a theory of education (using theory in the classical sense of *theoria*: the articulated perception of reality). He once remarked in passing: "Education should not try to relieve the other person of everything; it must have the humility to go along with what is the other person's [insight] and to help it mature."[7] This attitude was particularly evident in Ratzinger's supervision of his doctoral and postdoctoral candidates. He allowed each one of us to explore his chosen thesis with a freedom that was magnanimous, if not always easy on the student, since the personal responsibility involved could be truly demanding. The two terms just mentioned, freedom and personal responsibility, figure prominently in his later reflections on conscience, as we will see. For the moment it should suffice to say that they are intrinsic to the nature of truth, which could be described as the real passion in Ratzinger's life.

2. *The doctoral colloquium*

The doctoral colloquium, comprised of some thirty students at any one time, including visiting scholars, met once a fortnight during the semester.[8] It was an opportunity for a postgraduate to report on his research to date and to submit his tentative thesis to the (public) scrutiny of the professor and his fellow postgraduates. We convened every second Saturday in the Regensburg Diocesan Seminary— once the Irish Benedictine Abbey of Saint James. Each session began with concelebrated Mass, during which one

---

[7] *CEP* 60.

[8] For Ratzinger's own account of the colloquium, see *Salt of the Earth: Christianity and the Catholic Church at the End of the Millennium*, an interview with Peter Seewald [= *SE*], trans. Adrian Walker (San Francisco: Ignatius Press, 1992), p. 65. For a short history of the *Schülerkreistreffen* up to 1976, into which the original doctoral colloquium mutated, after Professor Ratzinger became Cardinal Archbishop of Munich in 1977, see Stephan Otto Horn, S.D.S., "Il Cardinale Ratziner e i suoi studenti", in Josef Clemens and Antonio Tarzia, eds., *Alla scuola della Verità: I settanta anni di Joseph Ratzinger* (Cinisello Balsamo [Milan]: San Paolo, 1997), pp. 9–26.

of the priest-students preached, and ended with lunch. At the end of the summer semester, this colloquium was expanded into a weekend session, to which some renowned theologian, such as Barth, von Balthasar, Rahner, or Pannenberg, was invited in order to discuss with us his most recent research or a particular theme for which he was particularly noted (such as inculturation or Greek Orthodox ecclesiology). The location was either somewhere convenient to the place of residence of the invited guest(s) or in a suitable house near Regensburg, such as a monastery or a conference center in the Alps. Invariably, the extended discussions took place in an atmosphere of conviviality, with time set aside for strolls through the inviting *Holzwege* of the Black Forest or the Bavarian Woods.

The doctoral colloquium was usually composed of a roughly equal number of German and non-German students from all over the world. As a result, a most stimulating forum was created. Due to Ratzinger's method of supervision, diversity prevailed. With the whole spectrum of theological opinions represented by the participants, a certain tension was unavoidable between the more "progressive" and the more "conservative" members. But all opinions were aired and respected, if subject to intense but invariably polite criticism. Ratzinger's own attitude was one of impartiality. Since truth is never found in its pure state here below, objectivity included the effort to distinguish between truth and its many falsifications. Later he was to remark that "All errors contain truths."[9] The motivating force of his whole theological enterprise is to uncover the truth, including those truths hidden in, and by, the great errors that have confronted the faith in its path through

---

[9] *TPE* 108.

history and that have also helped to clarify that faith. Understanding such errors can lead to a more profound grasp of the truth we call faith.

Ratzinger's approach also ensured that a certain lightness of touch, and occasional flashes of wit, marked these colloquia, despite their scholarly nature and the intensity of the discussion. After each session, opposing positions were forgotten and human relationships cemented. Humor marked the meals in common and the evening gathering over wine and beer. Perhaps one could say: *Ubi Ratzinger ibi hilaritas* (in Ratzinger's company cheerfulness prevailed): anecdotes abounded. Though reserved by nature—with a preference to listen to a good story—he is on occasion a gifted raconteur.

3. The lecturer

It was in his lectures, however, that Ratzinger primarily exercised his talent as a teacher, in the Greek understanding of that term. His auditors generally listened with rapt attention to the provisional findings of this one theologian's attempt to speak about God and the mysteries of the faith to the modern mind and thus to speak about the *humanum* in all its depth and richness. His lectures, like his seminars and colloquia, were not simply content with analysis and criticism. He also tried to articulate a new synthesis.[10] His findings were always provisional, open to new questions, new insights, corrections to earlier theories, and even misunderstandings. The theologian does not have the last word. That is the claim of Gnosis, perhaps the source of every heresy: the claim to know all truth.

[10] See *SE* 65.

What should one say to the accusation that Ratzinger later abandoned his earlier "progressive" views?[11] Whatever the suitability of using a term such as "progressive", Ratzinger did in fact develop his theology—and right up to his election as pope was still developing his insights, as we will see. He himself has also acknowledged mistakes he has made as a theologian.[12] And he would be happy to receive any other correction that might need to be made, since academic theology is of its nature explorative and thus tentative, open to revision and, so, development. He would surely agree with Newman, who, speaking about progress in thought, recognized that, "In a higher world it is otherwise, but here below to live is to change, and to be perfect is to have changed often."[13] Yet, there is an underlying consistency in all his writings that is more significant than any changes in detail. He himself has also drawn attention to the fact that, though he has remained basically the same in his theology, the situation in which he finds himself has changed. The nature of that inner consistency is hinted at in a theme he has several times explored, namely, education.

[11] It would seem that the discussion surrounding the draft text for what became *Gaudium et Spes*, the Pastoral Constitution on the Church in the Modern World, did indeed mark a significant turning point, to judge from Ratzinger's criticism of the basic thrust of the draft text, in particular its vulgarized *Teilhardisme*, which tended almost to identify human progress and Christian hope; cf. Aidan Nichols, O.P., *The Thought of Joseph Ratzinger: An Introduction to the Theology of Joseph Ratzinger* (London: Burns and Oates, 2005), pp. 99–103, who refers to Ratzinger's *Die letzte Sitzungsperiode des Konzils* (Cologne, 1966); English trans., *Theological Highlights of Vatican II* (New York: Paulist Press, 1966).

[12] See, for example, *Daughter Zion: Meditations on the Church's Marian Belief*, trans. John M. McDermott, S.J. (San Francisco: Ignatius Press, 1983), p. 51, n. 11, where he accepts criticism by von Balthasar of a possible misunderstanding arising from an earlier opinion on the Virgin Birth.

[13] John Henry Cardinal Newman, *An Essay in the Development of Christian Doctrine* (London: Longmans, Green, 1900), p. 40.

Speaking about the Church's contribution to peace and justice, Ratzinger points out that the Church's primary task is "education", as understood by the Greek philosophers. "She must break open the prism of positivism and awaken man's receptivity to the truth, to God, and thus to the power of conscience." [14] This understanding of the Church's role is at the core of his own philosophy of politics, according to which the Church "must give men the courage to live according to conscience and so keep open the narrow pass between anarchy and tyranny, which is none other than the narrow way of peace." [15] In his theology, moreover, it is the key to his methodology and, one may add, to his freedom of courage as a theologian. As we will see, Ratzinger demonstrates how frankness (or boldness) is an essential component of that biblical understanding of freedom which truth engenders in the human heart: "The apostle's frankness consists of saying the truth to a world dominated by appearance, even though this involves him in conflict (1 Thess 2:2)." [16] Ratzinger is no stranger to that conflict.

Later Ratzinger would have occasion to discuss the nature of academic life and its freedom, essential to which are dialogue based on listening, [17] freedom founded on truth, without any consideration of personal advantage, and cult

[14] *TPE* 55; see also *CEP* 263, 254.
[15] *TPE* 55.
[16] *CEP* 200.
[17] In his foreword to *Turning towards the Lord: Orientation in Liturgical Prayer*, by U. M. Lang (San Francisco: Ignatius Press, 2004), p. 10, the then Cardinal Ratzinger appealed for a more relaxed discussion on the question than was the case in the immediate aftermath of Vatican II. The quest for "the best ways of putting into practice the mystery of salvation" is to be achieved, he claimed, "not by condemning one another, but by carefully listening to each other and, even more importantly, listening to the internal guidance of the liturgy itself."

(adoration) as the end and guarantee of freedom.[18] This *theoria* corresponds to his lifelong *praxis*.

4. *The interaction of scholarship and contemporary events*

At the beginning of each semester, students of all years (and often from various disciplines) poured into one of the larger lecture halls to listen attentively to Joseph Ratzinger's introductory lectures. These were always remarkable. He began whatever tract he happened to be dealing with in that semester (for example, creation, Christology, or ecclesiology) by situating the subject matter first within the contemporary cultural context and then within the most recent theological developments, before going on to offer his own original, scholarly, and highly systematic examination of the topic.[19] In this, he was very much a *German* theologian, heir to, and an original contributor to, a rich tradition of theological scholarship (both Protestant and Catholic) at home in the university. Theology was forced to confront the radical thinking that first emerged there and to a great extent shaped the modern world. Ratzinger is therefore in many ways a controversial thinker and writer. He is controversial in the double sense that, first, the greater part of his writing has been in response to the controversies of the moment—most theological issues being at the same time issues of immediate relevance to contemporary society—while, secondly, many of his own theses in turn have given rise to controversy. Each of his writings bears the mark of one struggling to be true to the concerns of his fellow

[18] "On the Essence of the Academy and Its Freedom", in his collection of essays *The Nature and Mission of Theology* [= *NMT*], trans. Adrian Walker (San Francisco: Ignatius Press, 1995), pp. 31–41.

[19] The opening chapter of his *Introduction to Christianity*, entitled "Belief in the World of Today" is a good example of this style.

scholars while at the same time endeavoring to be true to God's self-revelation in Christ. One is reminded of 1 Peter 3:15, which exhorts us to give reasons for the hope that is in us. This text, he tells us in his *Memoirs*, provided the motivation for the young Ratzinger when he started his theological studies, just as it did for the great mediaeval theologians. In this, he is also true to Saint Augustine—the first object of his study—whose theology is an attempt to answer not only his own questions but especially those posed by the epoch-making events of which he was a part and which made the Bishop of Hippo in North Africa the Father of Western civilization for better and, indeed, for worse.

Ratzinger's own life has been marked by several epoch-making events, including the Second World War and its aftermath as well as the collapse of the Communist world, symbolized by the fall of the Berlin Wall, not to mention the revolution in biotechnology, all of which he has confronted in his writings. The most significant event of recent Church history was, undoubtedly, the Second Vatican Council. Archbishop Josef Cardinal Frings of Cologne, one of the most influential bishops at the Council, appointed Ratzinger (then thirty-six and only recently appointed professor at Bonn) as his *peritus* (expert theological advisor).[20] Together

---

[20] The aged Cardinal Frings met Ratzinger at a concert and invited the young professor, who had already earned something of a reputation, to help him with a talk he was invited to give at Genoa on November 20, 1961, in preparation for the Council. The Cardinal was so pleased with the text Ratzinger prepared that he made only one slight adjustment to it. The talk made quite an impression in Genoa. When Frings showed the text to Cardinal Julius Döpfner of Munich, the latter commented: "'Whew, a historical document', which Frings interpreted to mean: Those are dreams for the future, few of which will be realized" (Norbert Trippen, *Josef Kardinal Frings (1887–1978)*, vol. 2: *Sein Wirken für die Weltkirche und seine letzten Bischofsjahre* (Paderborn: Schöningh, 2005), pp. 240–41.

with Karl Rahner, S.J., and Hans Küng, Joseph Ratzinger soon began to exert that German influence which helped produce the exciting new and bold theology of the final documents. Other theological schools—notably the French (for example, Yves Congar, O.P., and Henri de Lubac, S.J.), Belgian (Msgr. G. Philips), Polish (Karol Wojtyła), and American (John Courtney Murray, S.J.)—had a profound effect on the Council's proceedings, in particular the final sessions, but it was the German liturgists and theologians, of whom Rahner, Ratzinger, and Küng were the most prominent, who gave rise to the title of a popular book by Ralph M. Wiltgen, S.V.D., intended as a description of what actually happened at the Council: *The Rhine Flows into the Tiber.*[21]

After the Council, Ratzinger, it seems to me, adopted a more critical approach to what he saw to be centrifugal forces unintentionally released by the Council[22] that began to undermine the original reforming thrust of the Council and soon became more and more extreme in their demands. *Concilium*, an international periodical published in various languages, became the main organ for the dissemination of the more radical interpretation of what was called "the spirit of Vatican II", marked by an anti-Roman bias and dissent

[21] New York: Hawthorn Books, 1967. For Ratzinger's own brief account of his time at the Council (apart from the books he wrote about the Council at the time), see *SE* 71ff., and *MM* 120ff. The theological differences between Ratzinger and Küng are known; less well known are the differences between Ratzinger and Rahner. "As we worked together [at the Council on the "Sources of Revelation" text], it became obvious to me that, despite our agreement in many desires and conclusions, Rahner and I lived on two different theological planets" (*MM* 128).

[22] See the epilogue to *Principles of Catholic Theology*, pp. 367–93, for Ratzinger's review of the postconciliar era and his inquiry into the reception of *Gaudium et Spes*.

from aspects of traditional Church teaching.[23] To counteract these currents of thought, Ratzinger, together with the
great Swiss theologian Hans Urs von Balthasar, the French
Jesuit Henri de Lubac, and others, founded an alternative
periodical, *Communio*, which is also published in various
language editions worldwide. This new international periodical of the highest scholarly standard is characterized by
its ethos of *sentire cum ecclesia*, that is, thinking with the
Church, remaining true to both tradition and contemporary Church teaching while engaging in an open yet critical dialogue with the world.

5. *Scholarship and Magisterium*

A growing pastoral concern, evident in Ratzinger's writings from the beginning, but more evident after the Council,[24] became the hallmark of many of his writings after his

[23] In his address to the Roman Curia on December 22, 2005, in which he
reviewed the major events of the previous year, Pope Benedict XVI also
commented on the fortieth anniversary of the closing of the Second Vatican
Council. The address contains his judgment of the great tasks that the Council set for itself and how its documents were implemented. The Council, he
points out, was implemented in two different ways corresponding to two
different interpretations: the hermeneutics of discontinuity and rupture, on
the one hand, and the hermeneutics of reform, on the other. The former
only accepted as authentic the "spirit" or progressive *thrust* of the documents
and so rejected any elements of the older tradition found in the texts, which
were regarded as compromises and so not binding. The latter interpreted the
Council—correctly in the Pope's view—within the context of the entire tradition, not as a rupture with tradition.

[24] I refer here in particular to the way his theology is always done in a
dialogue with contemporary events and currents of thought. His pastoral
touch is best seen in his preaching, as, for example, in the three programmatic
sermons he gave in Münster (Westphalia) during Advent 1964, recently
reprinted under the title *Vom Sinn des Christseins: Drei Adventspredigten* (Munich,
2005).

appointment by Pope Paul VI in 1977 as Archbishop of Munich and, soon after, Cardinal.[25] He still found time for research and publication of a more academic nature, and he continues (to this day) to enjoy the title of Professor of Dogma and the History of Dogma on the Faculty of Catholic Theology, University of Regensburg, originally in order to supervise those of his doctoral students (including this writer) who had yet to complete their dissertations. Even as Prefect of the Congregation for the Doctrine of the Faith, Joseph Cardinal Ratzinger continued to function as a professional theologian, albeit in a personal, nonofficial capacity, as it were. Through numerous public lectures and publications during his period as cardinal prefect, he continued to enter into debate with other theologians on equal terms. To the best of my knowledge, he is the only cardinal prefect in recent times to do so—and it is clear from his new book on Christology that as pope he will continue to do so, as indeed Pope John Paul II did with the publication of a number of his own personal writings.

It is therefore important to distinguish between official statements that carry his signature—then as cardinal prefect, now as pope—and his own writings as a great thinker or intellectual in the European tradition. Statements issued by the Congregation are part of the authoritative Magisterium, or teaching authority, of the Church. But the theses he proposes as a writer and thinker carry a different

[25] See, for example, his meditations for Advent and Christmastide, recently republished in *Der Segen der Weihnacht: Meditationen* (Freiburg im Breisgau: Herder, 2005), which combine scholarly insight with pastoral and spiritual intuition. See also his Lenten series of lectures on creation delivered in the Liebfrauenkirche, Munich, while he was archbishop there: *"In the Beginning . . .": A Catholic Understanding of the Story of Creation and the Fall*, trans. Boniface Ramsey, O.P. (Grand Rapids, Mich.: Eerdmans, 1995).

authority, that of any thinker or scholar, philosopher or theologian, namely, that based on the strength of the arguments he uses—and no more. Furthermore, as already mentioned, his thinking on various subjects has changed and matured with time (for example, on eschatology and on the sacrificial nature of the Eucharist). Authoritative statements of the Magisterium, such as various *Instructions* or *Notifications* issued by the Congregation for the Doctrine of the Faith under his signature should not be considered as Ratzinger's own theology but rather as authoritative statements of Church teaching. As will be mentioned below, Ratzinger's own theological reflections on these particular topics were written, I suspect, as part of his preparation for the discussions held within the Congregation when a particular document was being drafted or were written in response to the controversies raised by the documents (such as *Dominus Iesus*).[26]

---

[26] For his own theological reflections on this topic, see Joseph Cardinal Ratzinger, *Truth and Tolerance: Christian Belief and World Religions* [= *TT*], trans. Henry Taylor (San Francisco: Ignatius Press, 2004).

Chapter Two

RATZINGER'S WRITINGS: AN OVERVIEW

God is the real central theme of my endeavors.

—*Joseph Cardinal Ratzinger, Salt of the Earth*

Joseph Ratzinger is, to the best of my knowledge, the first academic theologian to fill the Shoes of the Fisherman, just as his immediate predecessor was the first professional philosopher to do so. Until his election as pope, he was one of the least known of the great German and French theologians who helped shape the Second Vatican Council. This is probably because of the way theology developed after the Council and the fact that, as already mentioned, while still a professor, Ratzinger cast

For an introduction to the theology of Joseph Ratzinger up to 1987, see Aidan Nichols O.P., *The Theology of Joseph Ratzinger: An Introductory Study* (Edinburgh, 1988), republished as *The Thought of Benedict XVI: An Introduction to the Theology of Joseph Ratzinger* (London: Burns and Oates, 2005), to which I am indebted, and Laurence Paul Hemming, *Benedict XVI: Fellow Worker for the Truth: An Introduction to His Life and Thought* (London: Burns and Oates, 2005). See the series of articles entitled "Joseph Ratzinger's Theological Ideas", by Jim Corkery, S.J., in *Doctrine & Life* 56 (2006), beginning with "1—Origins: A Theologian Emerges", in the February issue (pp. 6–14), and the dossier of articles published in *Kephas* (January–March 2006) entitled "Joseph Ratzinger au delà des clichés".

an increasingly cold eye on much that was to become theologically fashionable. Students of theology who quoted him were punished by their liberal professors, and those professors who did quote him—he is eminently quotable—would not reveal their source lest the insight be rejected. When he took on pastoral responsibilities as Archbishop of Munich and saw the devastating effect of some schools of theology on ordinary people's lives, he became more trenchantly critical. Finally, despite his best efforts to avoid higher appointment, he found himself eventually in the unenviable position of being made Prefect of the Congregation for the Doctrine of the Faith (hereafter CDF). His task for the next twenty-four years was to help re-identify what had become the somewhat porous boundaries that define our faith and to help clarify the Church's teaching in the face of new developments in science, philosophy, and politics. Understandably, he soon acquired the reputation of being the Grand Inquisitor, *Panzerkardinal*, or "enforcer of the faith"—and was presented by the media as practically the enemy of humanity. Again, this was not surprising, since the teaching of the Church on issues that affect us all in the depths of our being contradicts much that is fashionable.

Then, thanks to the media, came the turning point. When he presided at the Requiem Mass for Pope John Paul II and conducted his first appearances after his election as pope, people encountered a personality other than the one they thought they knew. This time they were seeing an image unfiltered by any editor—a shy, humble, but courageous man, whose spontaneous smile exuded warmth and joy and hope. But it was also a man who was no longer the customs officer who had to decide what was allowed entrance to the Church and what was not. He was now Christ's vicar on earth, the representative of him who is Love.

As pope, he has surprised many people, even professional theologians who had dismissed him without ever reading his writings or assumed that his theology was limited to the (sometimes poorly written) documents he signed as Prefect of the Congregation for the Doctrine of the Faith. Perhaps the most controversial document was *Dominus Iesus*, on the uniqueness and salvific universality of Jesus Christ and his Church, which unequivocally reiterated the doctrine that the one Church "subsists in" the Catholic Church, refused to use the term "Church" for Protestant denominations, and described all other religions as "objectively gravely deficient". No doubt the content of such documents did betray his inspiration. But those documents do not represent his theology; they are the Church's authoritative statements on matters of faith and morals—the source of and the parameters within which theology operates. Theology is something distinctly other. It is an attempt to discover the inner logic of that faith, to situate the faith within the questioning of the world's great thinkers and the existential situation of today, to discover (insofar as limited mortals can) what is *God's view* of reality and the human condition. Many professional theologians were unaware that Ratzinger had continued to write and publish as a private theologian while archbishop and later as prefect. But it is in those writings (together with his earlier, more scholarly works) that we find his own theology, his faltering but nonetheless stimulating insights into God's word as a response to the crucial questions affecting humanity individually and collectively.

1. Ratzinger's theological methodology

To appreciate Ratzinger's writings, one has to remember that all of his published material, official or private—and it covers a breathtaking scope of topics—is written from an explicitly theological perspective. In other words, it is argued in the light of reason *and* revelation, revelation as found in Scripture and tradition being the ultimate criterion. His theology is marked, first of all, by attention to the whole history of human questioning (philosophy) up to and including those questions articulated or implied by the situation in which we find ourselves today. Second, this theology is characterized by attention to the answers—often partial and inadequate ones—given in the course of history by the great thinkers of mankind, theologians and otherwise. Third, and most important, his theology is given its definitive form by its attempt to hear and interpret God's revelation of himself in Jesus Christ, that is, his design for mankind entrusted to the Church and testified to by Scripture read in the light of the history of dogma.[1]

I have just mentioned the word "history" three times. This is no accident. One of Ratzinger's basic methodological principles—following the examples of Plato, Aristotle, Augustine, and Aquinas—is that no serious philosophical or theological question can ever be adequately posed or answered, however tentatively, if the philosopher or theologian does not listen to the objections to it; and this implies being at least to some degree aware of the history of the question (and of the prior attempts made to answer it). Even more significant for Ratzinger is the need for every Christian—and, a fortiori, the theologian—to face facts squarely and not avoid what appears to be distinctly unpalatable or even at variance with his assumptions about the content of the faith.[2] Those assumptions might, in

---

[1] Ratzinger himself has noted that his point of departure is first of all the Word. "That we believe the word of God, that we try really to get to know it and understand it, and then, as I said, to think it together with the great masters of the faith. This gives my theology a somewhat biblical character and also bears the stamp of the Fathers, especially Augustine" (*SE* 66).

[2] Cf. Joseph Ratzinger, *Vom Sinn des Christseins: Drei Adventspredigten* (1965; Munich: Kösel, 2005), pp. 21–22.

fact, have to be revised, which is one of the tasks of the systematic theologian. All of Ratzinger's writings betray the courage to face any question or objection because of the confidence he has in the truth revealed in Jesus Christ and handed on by the Church's apostolic tradition.

The characteristics of all of Ratzinger's writing are his originality, creativity, and independence as a thinker. His more recent forays into moral theology and political science, though rooted in his early research in the history of dogma, are those of an original thinker conscious that his contribution to contemporary discourse is precisely that of a theologian. What I propose to do in the rest of this introduction is to provide an overview of his more important writings, beginning with his early publications.[3] Before doing so, I would like to draw the reader's attention to some of the major characteristics of his writings as well as to discuss the foundational research he carried out for his doctoral and postdoctoral dissertations, on which the entire edifice of his later writings is based.

2. *Some major characteristics*[4]

Truth and Tolerance[5] is Cardinal Ratzinger's 284-page answer to the worldwide outrage at the publication of *Dominus Iesus*

---

[3] It is difficult to give an overview of Ratzinger's publications considering the vast scope of his subject matter, the fragmentary nature of most of his writings, and the sheer volume of publications: some 86 books, 471 articles and prefaces, and 32 contributions to various encyclopedias and dictionaries. Regarding the bibliography of his writings, see above, p. 15, note 6. What follows must of its very nature be restricted to some of his more representative scholarly writings.

[4] The following first appeared as part of "The Mind of Benedict XVI" in the *Claremont Review of Books* (Fall 2005) and is reproduced here with the permission of the editors.

[5] *Glaube—Wahrheit—Toleranz* (Freiburg im Breisgau: Herder, 2003); English trans., *TT*.

(August 6, 2000), the document issued by the Congregation for the Doctrine of the Faith, of which he was prefect at the time. The document affirmed the absolute claims of Christianity and the Catholic Church vis-à-vis other religions. In the preface of his book, he wrote: "As I looked through my lectures on [Christian belief and world religions] from the past decade, it emerged that these approaches . . . amounted to something like a single whole—quite fragmentary and unfinished, of course, but, as a contribution to a major theme that affects us all, perhaps not entirely unhelpful" (p. 10). These sentiments highlight not only the dominant characteristic of the man—his humility and courage—but also the nature of most of his writings. They are fragmentary and mostly unfinished, but, taken together, they nonetheless constitute a single, unified body of work.

Ratzinger is conscious of the fragmentary nature of all he has written, but he makes a virtue out of this "weakness". Of course the fact that he was called to sacrifice the preferred life of an academic to serve the Church, first as Archbishop of Munich, then as prefect of the CDF, and now, of course, as pope, has meant that he has not had the leisure to write monographs. But in addition to this, as he says in one of his most recent publications, *Values in a Time of Upheaval*,[6] "perhaps it is precisely the incomplete character of these essays that may provide a spur to further thinking on these subjects." Like his university lectures, all of his writings are contributions to an ongoing debate, first the scholarly debate within his own discipline—theology—and, later, as he became more pastor than scholar, the public debate about the future of society and, above all, the Church's role in it.

Ratzinger, however, is not simply an outstanding scholar, he is also an original thinker. The result is an inner consistency that marks all his writings, even while each individual piece stands on its own and never fails to surprise his readers with its freshness, originality, and depth.

There is, however, a deeper theological justification for the fragmentary nature of his writings. In his critique of the basic thrust of Karl Rahner's admittedly formidable theological system, Ratzinger pinpointed "the real problem with Rahner's synthesis". This is the fact that "he has attempted too much. He has, so to speak, sought for a philosophical and theological world formula on the basis of which the whole of reality can be deduced cohesively from necessary causes." [7] Such a concept is evidently contrary to the mystery of freedom. Hans Urs von Balthasar placed his own theology of history under the programmatic title of *Das Ganze im Fragment* (the whole in the fragment)—in conscious opposition to such a concept—"in order to emphasize in advance that it is not given to man to see and express the whole in itself; at best he can have but an intimation of it in the fragmentary, the positive, the particular." [8] Balthasar developed an "open system" in contrast with closed systems, such as that found in Rahner. Ratzinger, it seems, achieved something similar in an even more radically fragmentary form, dictated, as mentioned above, at least in part by the limitations of his pastoral responsibilities as archbishop and prefect.

---

[7] *PCT* 169. Science recognizes today that there can be no world formula, since even in the realm of nature, as Jacques Monod has pointed out, there is more than mere necessity. "*A fortiori*, there can be no spiritual world formula—that was also Hegel's basic error" (*PCT* 169). At the root of this problem is Rahner's understanding of freedom, which, according to Ratzinger, "is proper to idealistic philosophy, a concept that, in reality, is appropriate to the absolute Spirit—to God—but not to man" (*PCT* 169–70).

[8] *PCT* 169.

Ratzinger has been described as the consummate listener, and that is what he is, attentive to the voices of others, be they great or small, be they the great thinkers of the past or his serious critics of the present. He listens to anyone who has anything to say, including his students. But most of all, he has given ear to the contributions made by great thinkers down through the ages. This capacity to listen with discernment, combined with his phenomenal erudition, makes him a superb partner in dialogue. One such dialogue took place in the Catholic Academy of Munich on January 19, 2004, with the Neo-Marxist Jürgen Habermas of the Frankfurt School as his interlocutor. The main topic of the debate concerned the possibility of establishing those (objective) moral values needed for society to function justly, what Ratzinger called the "Prepolitical moral foundations of a free State." [9] Habermas, donning the mantle of the Enlightenment, claimed that reason alone would be sufficient to the task, while Ratzinger disagreed. Reason alone had in fact failed in the past (a reference to twentieth-century ideologies). Reason needs religion, the crucible of human experience and source of human wisdom, to complete the task. In his paper, Ratzinger drew attention to the way the universalist claims of both the Enlightenment and Christianity, which have also become universal in fact, are today questioned by other religious traditions that cannot be ignored but must also be brought into the debate aimed at establishing a moral consensus. The debate ended with the reciprocal recognition of the need for a "double process of apprenticeship" in which reason and religion would again learn to become dependent on each other. Habermas

---

[9] Cardinal Ratzinger's contribution is reprinted in his *Values in a Time of Upheaval*, chap. 2.

was reported to have been quite overwhelmed by the quality of the debate (cf. *Le Monde*, April 27, 2005).

Even when he was Professor of Dogmatic Theology with a large doctoral colloquium—on average some thirty doctoral and postdoctoral students at a time during his tenure at the University of Regensburg—one heard the reproach that he had failed to form a "school of theology", comparable, for example, to those propounded by the other two great modern German-speaking theologians, Karl Rahner and Hans Urs von Balthasar. Certainly the subject matter of the doctoral and postdoctoral theses he supervised covered the whole range of the history of dogma and systematic theology. This range of subjects reflects the comparably vast range of subjects he covered in his own *œuvre*. Though at home in systematic theology, he never set out to create a system or a "school of thought".[10] In that sense, he is a postmodern, but in fact he is more in tune with the first Christian thinkers, the Fathers of the Church. His theology is seminal in a way I would like to explore in the next few paragraphs.

3. *Liberal or conservative?*

In an interview after Benedict's election, Rodrigo Caviero of the *Correio Braziliense* asked me to account for what is generally assumed to be the transformation of the liberal theologian before the Second Vatican Council into Ratzinger the

[10] "I have never tried to create a system of my own, an individual theology. What is specific, if you want to call it that, is that I simply want to think in communion with the faith of the Church, and that means above all to think in communion with the great thinkers of the faith. The aim is not an isolated theology that I draw out of myself but one that opens as widely as possible into the common intellectual pathway of the faith" (*SE* 66).

conservative of more recent times. It is a question that many pose and one that I have dealt with in detail in another context.[11] It seems to me that placing great thinkers in pigeonholes often simply reflects unexamined prejudices. First as a professor and then as a cardinal, Joseph Ratzinger, in the course of his life as a theologian, developed a rich, mature body of writings, as we will see. His writings are incredibly dense, in need of unfolding and development. They are in fact "seminal", seeds of originality and creativity, which future generations will bring to completion. His insights into Christian faith and modern life are personally enriching and intellectually stimulating.

I can illustrate this through an experience I had teaching in the Regional Seminary of Papua New Guinea and the Solomon Islands. One of the topics I had to cover was the theology of the Christian sacraments. Following the methodology of Ratzinger, my *Doktorvater*, I sought for some starting point in the local culture, which is (broadly speaking) aboriginal and accordingly the happy hunting ground for anthropologists of all kinds, and in the theological confusion caused by botched attempts at the "inculturation" of the liturgy. Thanks to an anthropologist confrère, Father Jim Knight, S.V.D., I was introduced to the world of primitive rites—in particular, the studies of Victor Turner, who pioneered the anthropological study of ritual, and

---

[11] See "A Question of Fairness", *Homiletic & Pastoral Review* 102/1 (2001): 53–54. Due to the modern notion that salvation comes through change, Ratzinger once commented "... labeling a person conservative is practically synonymous with social excommunication, for it means, in today's language, that such a one is opposed to progress, closed to what is new and, consequently, a defender of the old, the obscure, the enslaving; that he is an enemy of the salvation that change is expected to bring about" (*PCT* 60); see his own analysis of progressivism in *PCT* 85ff.; also 395ff. (on the reception of Vatican II).

Mary Douglas, whose anthropology of natural symbols has thrown much light on contemporary developments in Church and society. I was also introduced to the world of comparative religion (in particular, Mircea Eliade). In my search for a theological framework with which to evaluate all that I had studied, it was Ratzinger who provided the hermeneutical key. I had brought with me to Papua New Guinea two thin pamphlets he had published on the notion of sacrament.[12] They not only provided me with the theological framework within which to evaluate contemporary primitive rites of initiation still practiced in Papua New Guinea and to situate them in the history of mankind that culminated in Christ. His insights also enabled me to appreciate the lasting significance of these rites and to relate them to the Old Testament and New Testament rites that resulted in the sacraments as we know them today. The ideas he had developed in the two pamphlets were seminal.

According to Ratzinger, the Christian sacraments are rooted in primordial human experiences that arise at crucial moments in life, namely, fertility, birth, the transition to manhood, to marriage, the assumption of leadership, and, finally, death, the transition to the beyond. Rites of passage were devised to deal with these liminal experiences, when man is most open to the beyond. These rites all share a

[12] Joseph Ratzinger, *Die sakramentale Begründung christlicher Existenz*, 3rd ed. (Meitingen and Freising: Kyrios Verlag, 1970). This is the text of a four-hour lecture that he delivered at the Salzburg Hochschulwoche in 1965. It is primarily concerned with finding a new approach to the reality of the sacraments and their central significance in a world that has lost touch with the sacramental dimension of Christian living. The second was a lecture given at the Catholic Theology Faculty of the University of Eichstätt on January 23, 1978, entitled *Zum Begriff des Sakramentes*, Eichstätter Hochschulreden 15 (Munich: Minerva, 1979). See also *PCT*, 27–30; 186; 240–42.

basic pattern, that of dying and rising to new life, such as to a new status in the community. These rites underwent a radical transformation during the history of salvation when they were associated with defining moments in that history, such as the Exodus. This transformation followed a dual process: a moment of demythologizing and an interpretative moment, central to which was the prophetic word (that became Scripture). It culminated in the central event of salvation history, the life, death, and Resurrection of God become man, Jesus Christ. In time, the Church developed rites around seven central passages from death to sin to new life in Christ, the seven sacraments. But the basic human experience, first articulated in the primitive rituals, remains the same. Ratzinger's insights, when implanted, as it were, in the humus of anthropology and comparative religion, helped me produce a rich crop of lectures, which, on my return to Europe, I delivered to an appreciative audience at the University of Fribourg (Switzerland) during the summer semester of 1984, when I was a visiting professor there.

From my own acquaintance with Professor Joseph Ratzinger, I can only attribute his perceived change from young liberal to old conservative to the fact that he is not simply a respected scholar and academic of international fame. He is an original thinker. It is undeniable that, before the Second Vatican Council, he was, compared with the established theology of the day, liberal and progressive, not to say revolutionary. He himself has said that his basic impulse, "precisely during the Council, was always to free up the authentic kernel of the faith from encrustations and to give this kernel strength and dynamism. This impulse is the constant of my life." [13] In that sense, he is a critical thinker.

[13] SE 79.

Like every profound thinker who has engaged with the great thinkers of most cultural traditions past and present (his erudition is astonishing), he is not only an astute observer of society and culture, but he has always maintained a critical distance toward both. This inner distance—born of his passion for truth, his lifelong search for the truth, and his capacity for self-criticism—enables him to appreciate and enter into dialogue with contemporary intellectual currents of thought, and especially theological thought, which latter touches on the most profound of all human questions. While many theologians remained, it could be said, stuck in the heady liberalism of the late 1960s, Ratzinger moved on—and so began to appear as a conservative or traditionalist, neither of which labels does justice to the man or his writings. He soon turned his critical mind to the new theological establishment, thinkers who are still in power in most faculties, though their day is now more or less over. His independent thinking brought him into conflict with those who were caught up in what used to be called "the spirit of Vatican II", which in subsequent years had turned into unthinking conformity with prevailing fashions.[14] To keep his independence as a thinker called for enormous character and courage (and wit)—helped by self-control in the face of his increasingly negative public image. That new image seemed hardly to bother him, convinced as he has always been of the long-term power of truth, which confidence likewise accounts for his own self-effacement.

This is not to deny that Ratzinger has changed certain of his views in the course of his long career. Change as such

[14] See his comments on the two different ways of interpreting the Council in note 23 of Chapter One.

is part of growth and a necessary condition for serious scholarly work, especially in the form of a readiness to be corrected, as when he accepted Balthasar's critique of his earlier view (expressed in *Introduction to Christianity*) that Jesus' divine sonship in itself would not exclude his descent from a normal marriage.[15] Change is also a prerequisite for authentic Christian living. As Dietrich von Hildebrand forcefully put it: "*Unreserved readiness* to change is the indispensable prerequisite for the reception of Christ into our soul", which Ratzinger quotes in his discussion of repentance.[16] In that context he refers approvingly to "the humorously ironic words" of the German popular writer Wilhelm Busch: "When you have lost your reputation, you are free to live your life without care." Ratzinger adds: The courage to break [with contemporary mores] is liberating—it also gives freedom.[17] Is he, perhaps, speaking from experience?

Ratzinger has never taken himself too seriously. He has always retained his humor.[18] This attitude of mind has been fostered by a consciousness that the truth is not something we create but something we discover and so stands on its own, irrespective of the person of the theologian. It is an

---

[15] Cf. Joseph Ratzinger, *Daughter Zion: Meditations on the Church's Marian Belief*, trans. John M. McDermott, S.J. (San Francisco: Ignatius Press, 1983), p. 51, n. 11.

[16] Quoted by Ratzinger in his discussion of change and constancy within the context of faith as conversion (metanoia), *PCT* 62.

[17] Cf. Ibid. The translation of Busch's aphorism is mine, as the published English translation does not quite do justice to the point made, though it does catch the rhyme: "Once your good name's undermined,/That's one worry off your mind."

[18] "Where joylessness reigns, where humor dies, the spirit of Jesus Christ is assuredly absent" (*PCT* 84). The context of this statement relates to the nature of Christian joy, a central concern of Ratzinger's writings and in his sermons and talks as pope (see Joseph Murphy, *An Invitation to Joy: The Theological Vision of Pope Benedict XVI* [San Francisco: Ignatius Press, 2007]).

attitude that has helped to keep him in constant dialogue with those who have disagreed with him, trying to see their point of view, engaging in self-criticism (thereby remaining open to correction), and finding new ways to appeal to them. He seeks dialogue and understanding. He is concerned with the truth, which alone can make us (as individuals and as a society) free, the freedom of love that engenders hope and joy.

4. *Foundational research*

From the beginning of his own studies, he and many contemporaries in Munich tended to seek an alternative to what had been the dominant system of Catholic theology up to then, Neo-Scholasticism. The latter was an attempt in the nineteenth and early twentieth centuries to re-create the mediaeval philosophical and theological system of Saint Thomas Aquinas. It was, we can say in hindsight, an effort marred by the very rationalism it tried to overcome. Instead, Ratzinger turned to the great thinkers of the early Church. For his doctoral thesis, he studied *the* Father of the Western Church—and of Western civilization—Saint Augustine of Hippo in North Africa. Though he recognized the greatness of Scholasticism and its inner dialectic, which, properly understood, preserves the tension of that inner-theological debate that arises from a communal search for the truth, Ratzinger found this system of thought too impersonal. "With Augustine, however, the passionate, suffering, questioning man is always right there, and you can identify with him." [19]

His topic was Augustine's understanding of the Church—and thus, by implication, his understanding of the State

[19] *SE* 61.

and the political significance of Christianity. His dissertation, *Volk und Haus Gottes in Augustins Lehre von der Kirche* (People of God and God's house in Augustine's doctrine of the Church)[20] is a classic. (Unfortunately, it has not yet been translated into English.) It is also the root of much of his later theology. It inspired his contributions to the documents of the Second Vatican Council and provided the inspiration he later needed to combat various misunderstandings of the Council, not least the mistaken attempt to conceive the Church as the People of God in more or less empirical or sociological, not to say political, terms.

His postdoctoral dissertation was devoted to Saint Thomas Aquinas' contemporary Saint Bonaventure, who was also very much in the Augustinian tradition. Entitled *The Theology of History in St. Bonaventure*,[21] it is an analysis of the attempt by the great Franciscan theologian to come to terms with the then-new understanding of history conceived by the Abbot Joachim of Fiore (ca. 1135–1202). The latter's essentially Gnostic speculations were taken up by some of the followers of Saint Francis, known as the Spirituals, whose radical interpretation of Franciscan poverty, combined with a Joachimite apocalyptic interpretation of history, made them the first revolutionary movement of the second millennium. Their goal was to usher in a new age marked by a spiritual brotherhood of all men. They split the early Franciscans in two and forced Bonaventure, the Master General of the young Franciscan Congregation, to address Joachim's theories.

---

[20] Munich: Zink, 1954.

[21] *Die Geschichtstheologie des heiligen Bonaventura* (1959), English trans. by Zachary Hayes (Chicago: Franciscan Herald Press, 1971). For Ratzinger's own evaluation of the significance of his study of Bonaventure, see *SE* 61–63.

As Eric Voegelin has shown,[22] the speculations of Joachim of Fiore are in large part the source of modernity. They effectively helped replace the Augustinian concept of history that had informed Western Christendom up to then, namely, that history was something *transitory*, the rise and fall of empires. Empires pass away; only the eternal *Civitas Dei* (the "citizenry of God", as Ratzinger translates it) lasts forever. Its sacramental expression is the Church, understood as mankind in the process of redemption. Joachim proposed an exciting new conception of world history as a divine *progression* within three distinct eras, that of the Father (the Old Testament, or the period of the laity or patriarchs), that of the Son (the Church since the New Testament, or the period of the clerics), and a third era, that of the Holy Spirit, the period of the ascetic monks or spirituals, which was about to break into history. In

---

[22] See especially Eric Voegelin, *The New Science of Politics: An Introduction* (Chicago and London: University of Chicago Press, 1952), chap. 4, in particular, pp. 111–27. I had often noted the way Ratzinger's theology of politics echoed central themes common to Voegelin but did not suspect any direct influence, despite the occasional reference to Voegelin in Ratzinger's published *oeuvre* (for example, *Die Einheit der Nationen: Eine Vision der Kirchenväter* [Salzburg and Munich: Pustet, 1971, reprinted 2005], p. 25; *Der Gott Jesu Christi: Betrachtungen über den Dreieinigen Gott* [Munich: Kösel, 1976], p. 36). Recently, a colleague here in Maynooth, Thomas Norris, gave me a copy of a letter from Ratzinger, when he was Archbishop of Munich, to Eric Voegelin, thanking the latter for a book with a personal dedication, which he had received together with an invitation to a celebration to mark Voegelin's eightieth birthday. "It was as great a surprise as it was a joy for me to receive your philosophical meditation, which you kindly sent to me with a personal dedication, in which you intend to awaken such a necessary and such a very fragile consciousness of the imperfect in opposition to the magic of the Utopian. Ever since your small book *Science, Politics and Gnosticism* came into my hands in 1959, your thinking has fascinated and stimulated me, even though I was unfortunately unable to study it with the thoroughness I would have wished."

the third period, all structures (Church and State) would give way to the perfect society of autonomous men moved only from within by the Spirit. This understanding of history is based on what Voegelin calls "the immanentization of the eschaton", in other words, the assumption that the end of history is immanent to itself, is an inner-worldly manifestation, the product of history's own inner movement toward ever greater perfection, the kingdom of God *on earth*. It is at the root of what we mean today by "progress". It underpins, albeit in different ways, both radical socialism and liberal capitalism. And it has had a profound effect on political life, giving rise to both revolution and secularism.

Bonaventure, according to Ratzinger, failed in his critique; it was not radical enough. It was, however, significant for Ratzinger's future engagement with political thought since his sensitivity to the philosophical and theological issues underlying contemporary political life were fine-tuned by his study of Bonaventure. This is seen in particular in his later treatment of the extreme forms of liberation theology based on a Marxist notion of history that has its deepest roots in the speculations of Joachim of Fiore.

5. The early period

As a professional German academic, first in Freising and then in Bonn, Ratzinger's early writings were devoted to fundamental theology, that is, systematic reflection on the basic principles and presuppositions of theology. The subjects covered included the nature of theology as *Wissenschaft* (science, or scholarship), the meaning of Christian revelation and, so, of tradition, as well as the nature of the Church (that is, ecclesiology). Related subjects he treated included ecumenism and the broader question of the relationship between the Church and the world religions, with particular attention to the relationship between Christianity and Judaism. Ratzinger stresses the affinity between reason and revelation (and, thus, the Church's appreciation of philosophy as an ally in her enlightened critique of myth both in antiquity and today). For Ratzinger, "reason" is our capacity for truth (and, therefore, for God). Like language, reason is at the same time both personal and communal by nature. Indeed, so is revelation, the social dimension of which is found in the human-divine complex of tradition/Church. Ratzinger's entire theological opus is rooted in Scripture, the ultimate norm of all theology, judiciously interpreted using the findings of modern exegesis.[23] However, his scriptural interpretation goes beyond modern critical scholarship and is inspired by the example of the Church Fathers, whose own interpretation of Scripture is based on the unity of the Old and New Testaments (the latter seen as the fulfillment of the former) and the unfolding of tradition under the direction of the Holy Spirit down to our day.[24]

[23] "The historicocritical method is a marvelous instrument for reading historical sources and interpreting texts" (*TT* 133). His basic criticism is that underlying much historico-critical study of *Scripture* are philosophical assumptions of a positivistic nature that are inimical to the very content of Scripture. Since they are generally not subject to any self-criticism, they can lead exegetes to conclusions that are unacceptable. Though these findings may be presented as objective or scientific, they generally reflect more the unquestioned assumptions of the exegete (133–36). See also his comments in *MM* 127.

[24] See his "Biblical Interpretation in Crisis: On the Question of the Foundations and Approaches of Exegesis Today. Erasmus Lecture 1988" in *This World: A Journal of Religion and Public Life* 22 (Summer 1988): 1–19; for an extended version of this text, see Joseph Ratzinger, ed., *Schriftauslegung im Widerstreit*, Quaestiones Disputatae 117 (Freiburg im Breisgau: Herder, 1989), pp. 7–44.

Ratzinger's early period was greatly influenced by the Second Vatican Council and its consequences. He published several commentaries on texts issued by the Council as well as personal reflections on the four sessions of the Council and on its aftermath. Dealing with the vexing question of the universal nature of salvation and the particular nature of the Church, which the Council had posed with renewed sharpness and which was often expressed in terms of Karl Rahner's catchphrase "anonymous Christianity,"[25] Ratzinger developed his understanding of salvation in terms of *Stellvertretung* (representation/substitution). According to this, if I understand him correctly, the Church continues to make effective in each generation the salvific action of Christ on the Cross by which he redeemed the world. Just as the incarnate Word of God gave his life "for the many", so, too, individual Christians must live, not for themselves, but for others, while the Church exists, not for herself, but for the rest of mankind and thus enables Christ's grace to transform all those outside the visible Church who follow the deepest stirrings of their conscience. His major writings in this area include *Revelation and Tradition*,[26] *Das neue Volk Gottes*

[25] According to Rahner, all religions embody salvific values that, in principle, enable those adherents to become recipients of grace. All, therefore, who receive divine grace can be described as anonymous Christians, since all grace comes through the one Mediator, Jesus Christ (1 Tim 2:5). What is *implicitly* true for redeemed mankind has, Rahner claims, become *explicit* in Christianity. For a succinct and critical account of Rahner's later theory and its implications both for Western liberal theology and for liberation theology, see Walter Kasper, "Nature, Grace, and Culture: On the Meaning of Secularization" in David L. Schindler, ed., *Catholicism and Secularization in America* (Huntington, Ind.: Our Sunday Visitor; Notre Dame, Ind: Communio Books, 1990), pp. 42–44.

[26] *Offenbarung und Überlieferung*, with Karl Rahner (Freiburg im Breisgau: Herder, 1965); English trans. by W.J. O'Hara (New York: Herder and Herder, 1966).

(The new people of God),[27] and the *Principles of Catholic Theology*,[28] perhaps his most important academic writing.

Principles of Catholic Theology is in effect an attempt to place what was called, in the language of the specialist, fundamental (dogmatic) theology on a new footing. Fundamental theology is concerned with the formal principles of theology, the underlying assumptions arising from the nature of reason and revelation that are needed to reflect on the data of revelation and the nature of the human condition. The subtitle is revealing: "Building Stones for a Fundamental Theology". It is a collection of articles published between the late 1960s and the late 1970s, fragments now arranged in such a way as to constitute a whole, yet leaving each "building stone" unfinished, inviting completion by future generations of theologians. It is remarkable not only for its pastoral motivation and academic erudition (including a judicious use of world literature), but also for its broad ecumenical perspective. In his concluding remarks on his discussion of the influence of the initially Protestant (mostly Lutheran) concept of the "history of salvation" on the more metaphysical Catholic concept of salvation, he states, on the one hand, that "Catholic theology in its reflections needs the dialogue with Protestant theology; that, despite all divisions and conflict, there is a common theological fate; that both sides, whether in receiving or rejecting each other's position, are indeed always related and are defined by each other." On the other hand, he rejects any simple acceptance of whatever happens to be the stronger system and advocates a search for the common

---

[27] *Das neue Volk Gottes: Entwürfe zur Ekklesiologie* (Düsseldorf: Patmos, 1969).
[28] *Theologische Prinzipienlehre* (Munich: Wewel, 1982); English trans. by Sister Mary Frances McCarthy, S.N.D. (San Francisco: Ignatius Press, 1987).

ground, though each side should not to be shy to take any correction the other partner has to offer.[29] The English title of the book is somewhat misleading (*Principles of Catholic Theology*), as the original title is *Theologische Prinzipienlehre*, without any mention of "Catholic", though the work *is* catholic in the broadest sense of the term, namely, all-embracing.

At the core of this work, it seems to me, is Ratzinger's analysis of the central thrust of Rahner's theology, already mentioned above. Indeed, the book as a whole could be interpreted as Ratzinger's answer to Rahner's (closed) system, which in effect reduced theology to *one* fundamental formal principle, the "supernatural existential". This sees "human subjectivity as functioning within a horizon of being whose ultimate determinant is God".[30] Ratzinger's achievement is to restore to fundamental theology its differentiated principles, which enrich theological reflection and promote true progress in theology.

6. The middle period

Before looking at what might be called Ratzinger's middle period, I want to acknowledge that such divisions are somewhat artificial. There is also a danger that they might distract from an appreciation of the fundamental consistency in all of Ratzinger's writings. Thus, for example, in his final period, he returned to his earlier interests in fundamental theology in such books as *The Nature and Mission of*

---

[29] *PCT* 180–81 (my own translation from p. 189 of the German original, as the English version does not appear to me to be accurate).

[30] Article on Karl Rahner in F.L. Cross and E.A. Livingstone, eds., *The Oxford Dictionary of the Christian Church*, 3rd ed. (Oxford: Oxford University Press, 1997), p. 1362.

Theology[31] and *Called to Communion,*[32] which is a short course on ecclesiology, the fruit of his mature thinking. These works were greatly influenced by the more specific dogmatic concerns that occupied his attention during his middle period, when he taught dogmatic theology and the history of dogma, as well as by later pastoral challenges he encountered as archbishop and cardinal. Also of influence were the numerous doctoral theses he supervised.[33]

In all his writings, the Church is seen as a divine/human reality that constitutes a *communio*—that is, mankind in the process of becoming one. The source of that unity is the Eucharist, the sacrament of the Paschal Mystery by which God in Christ reunited sinful mankind with himself. Communion in and with the one Body and one Blood of Christ in the Eucharist transforms the faithful interiorly or spiritually into the one Body of Christ that is the Church, "Body of Christ" being the most distinctive New Testament and patristic description of the new People of God. But the Church is not just a spiritual reality. She is a visible entity, at once local and universal, a communion of communities,

---

[31] *Wesen und Auftrag der Theologie* (Einsiedeln: Johannes Verlag, 1993); English trans. by Adrian Walker (San Francisco: Ignatius Press, 1995).

[32] *Zur Gemeinschaft gerufen* (Freiburg im Breisgau: Herder, 1991); English trans. by Adrian Walker (San Francisco: Ignatius Press, 1996).

[33] These include Vincenz Pfnür on the recognition on the part of the Catholic Church of the (Lutheran) *Confessio Augustana* and the theology of justification; Siegfried Wiedenhoffer on Melanchton and political theology; G. Linde on Albert Camus; Martin Trimpe on the theology of the Petrine ministry of the Bishop of Rome, according to the sixteenth-century England of Cardinal Reginald Pole; Stephan Otto Horn on Pope Leo the Great and the Council of Chalcedon. Père Bartholomé Adoukonou's thesis on a Christian hermeneutic of Dahomian Voodoo influenced Ratzinger's theology of religions and their relationship to the Paschal Mystery, while he draws on Frederick Hartl's postdoctoral thesis on Ernst Block and Franz von Baader in his analysis of neo-Marxism. And there are many others.

whose visible unity is manifested and guaranteed by the apostolic succession in union with the Petrine ministry of the Bishop of Rome. The goal of the Church, her basic mission, is the the incorporation of man into the life-rhythm of the Trinitarian God.

In this middle period (as Professor of Dogma and History of Dogma at the Universities of Münster, Tübingen, and Regensburg), Ratzinger's most famous book of all was produced, *Introduction to Christianity*,[34] which has since been translated into some nineteen languages, including Arabic and Chinese. His creative thinking on the nature of sacrament, developed in small but significant essays such as that entitled *Die sakramentale Begründung christlicher Existenz* (The sacramental basis of Christian existence),[35] has yet to be absorbed into mainstream sacramental theology, as far as I can see. That particular book has not even been translated into English. His thinking on the nature of the Church was enriched by his reflections on the specifically dogmatic themes of creation, Christology, Trinity, and eschatology, as well his early reflections on the Eucharist and the nature of the liturgy, such as *The Feast of Faith: Approaches to a Theology of the Liturgy*.[36]

Most of his writings on the Church's dogmas have been occasional contributions to an ongoing debate and are thus of an increasingly fragmentary nature. Some of the principal works are to be found in the collection entitled *Dogma*

[34] *Einführung in das Christentum* (Munich: Kösel Verlag, 1968; rev. ed., 2000); English trans. by J. R. Foster (London: Burns and Oates, 1969; rev. ed.: San Francisco: Ignatius Press, 2004).

[35] *Die sakramentale Begründung christlicher Existenz* (Meitingen and Freising: Kyrios Verlag, 1966).

[36] *Das Fest des Glaubens* (Einsiedeln: Johannes Verlag, 1981); English trans. by Graham Harrison (San Francisco: Ignatius Press, 1986).

and Preaching.[37] Also of note are his short books *The God of Jesus Christ: Meditations on God in the Trinity,*[38] *"In the beginning . . .": A Catholic Understanding of the Story of Creation and the Fall* (four sermons),[39] and *Daughter Zion,*[40] his major (but not his only) contribution to Mariology.

The most significant book of this period is perhaps his *Eschatology: Death and Eternal Life,*[41] which is a well-worked-out, systematic textbook. This period is also marked by his growing concern with developments in catechesis, the handing on of the faith in schools and colleges, as reflected in the talk "Sources and Transmissions of the Faith,"[42] which he gave in France and which caused quite a storm at the time. These critical reflections on the contemporary situation of catechesis and on the basic principles of catechesis prepared him for his work as chairman of the commission set up by Pope John Paul II to oversee the composition of the *Catechism of the Catholic Church*, perhaps the most significant achievement of that pontificate.

[37] *Dogma und Verkündigung* (Munich: Wewel, 1973); English trans. by Matthew J. O'Connell (Chicago: Franciscan Herald Press, 1985).

[38] *Der Gott Jesu Christi: Betrachtungen über den Dreieinigen Gott* (Munich: Kösel, 1976); English trans. by Robert J. Cunningham (Chicago: Franciscan Herald Press, 1979).

[39] *Im Anfang schuf Gott* (Munich: Wewel, 1986); English trans. by Boniface Ramsey, O.P. (Huntington, Ind.: Our Sunday Visitor, 1990; rev. and enlarged ed., Grand Rapids, Mich.: Eerdmans, 1995).

[40] *Die Tochter Zion* (Einsiedeln: Johannes Verlag, 1977); English trans. by John M. McDermott, S.J. (San Francisco: Ignatius Press, 1983).

[41] *Eschatologie—Tod und ewiges Leben* (Regensburg: Pustet, 1977); English trans. by Michael Waldstein (Washington, D.C.: Catholic University of America Press, 1988).

[42] "Transmission de la foi et sources de la foi", in D.J. Ryan et al., *Transmettre la foi aujourd'hui* (Paris: Centurion, 1983); English trans. in *Communio: International Catholic Review* 10 (1983): 17–34.

7. *The later period*

As already mentioned, Ratzinger, now Cardinal Prefect of the Congregation for the Doctrine of the Faith, continued to do research and publish in academic journals. Though these writings must be regarded as quite distinct from the official documents that carried his signature, the two categories of writing, as already mentioned, were often related to each other. His scholarly writings were sometimes part of his preparation for the drawing up of official documents or were later reflections on those documents, in particular on their reception by the larger public, such as the extensive article that appeared in the *Frankfurter Allgemeine Zeitung* (September 22, 2000) responding to the controversy sparked by the publication of *Dominus Iesus*, which had stressed the absolute claims of Christ and the unity of his Church. His publications during this later period include various sermons, reflections, and spiritual exercises he gave as a bishop and pastor. All are marked by a deep spirituality, simplicity of language, and beauty of expression, such as *To Look on Christ: Exercises in Faith, Hope, and Love*.[43] His pastoral concern also produced some of his finest writings on the Eucharist, such as the article "Eucharist and Mission",[44] as well as the essays and sermons collected by Stephan Otto Horn and Vinzenz Pfnür in *God Is Near Us*.[45]

Ever since the Council, Ratzinger was concerned with the way theological debate had moved quite dramatically

---

[43] *Auf Christus schauen: Einübung in Glaube, Hoffnung, Liebe* (1989; new ed., Freiburg im Breisgau: Herder, 2006); English trans. by Robert Nowell (New York: Crossroad, 1991).

[44] *Irish Theological Quarterly* 65 (2000): 245–64.

[45] *Gott ist uns nah* (Augsburg: Sankt Ulrich Verlag, 2001); English trans. by Henry Taylor (San Francisco: Ignatius Press, 2003).

out of the university seminar into the media, which, to put it mildly, has never been the most ideal forum for theological debate. Theological ideas that had not yet matured were suddenly front-page news. Unused to any questioning of traditional doctrine, the public were suddenly confronted with interpretations that seemed to contradict their understanding of those doctrines. Unversed in academic theology, most of the faithful simply had to choose between the authority of the experts and the authority of what they had learned at school and from the pulpit. Many of these new theses have not stood the test of time, and yet they affected the lives of many, discouraging them, for example, from the often heroic effort needed to adhere to Catholic moral principles.

Debate among scholars is essential, but the most it can achieve is a temporary consensus, which can be replaced by a new, more compelling argument. Eventually what is of value in theological debate is incorporated into Church teaching by the authentic Magisterium (Church's teaching authority). At that stage, theologians have a different task, namely, to communicate these insights into the Church's doctrine to the public at large, to find a language and suitable images to convey truths that illuminate the human condition and enable us to engage in a critique of the dominant culture. But if the tentative theses of the theologians are presented to the public as "the last word" with full media coverage, then the result can only be confusing. This is what happened in the wake of the Council, when theologians were calling for their consensus at the time to be regarded as a kind of magisterium parallel to that of the pope and the bishops.

The resulting confusion among ordinary faithful, whose practice and devotion had already been shaken by the (necessary) reforms of Vatican II, was a real concern to

Ratzinger—and, I think, remains so. Theology should inspire and give hope, not cause confusion and despair. His sermons from his period as Cardinal Archbishop of Munich show a theologian capable of touching the hearts and minds of the faithful (something the world at large unexpectedly experienced for the first time when he preached at the obsequies for Pope John Paul II and, again, after his election as pope). His own theology at this later stage was marked by his new pastoral concerns in responding to a growing secularism he observed around him and a related weakening of confidence in Christian, Catholic values. He responded as well to certain developments in the reform of the liturgy that alarmed him, such as a growing arbitrariness vis-à-vis the Church's ritual. It was at this stage that he turned his attention to the question of the role of Christianity in a modern pluralist democracy and the breakdown of society in Europe as it collapses into the black hole created by the denial of the Absolute in public life. His podium was the pulpit, and his sermons and spiritual reflections from this period onward are in the tradition of the great Fathers of the Church, who forged their theology in answer to the needs of their flocks. His theological concerns were often dictated by current developments in politics and society in general but in particular by the pervasive moral relativism that undermines human well-being and erodes human communities.

As Prefect of the Congregation for the Doctrine of the Faith, his task was quite different. There he had to defend the parameters within which theology (including ethics) and Church life need to be conducted if they are to remain true to the Catholic and apostolic tradition. He had to do this in a rapidly changing world of high technology and political turmoil and in the context of a Church still reeling from the radical changes introduced by the Second Vatican Council. Developments in society and biotechnology created new social and moral dilemmas, which called for a refinement of traditional moral principles at a time when moral theology was in the process of renewing itself, a process that is only beginning to find some kind of closure. Put simply, the Council called for a reform of moral theology, which up to then had been too legalistic (indeed, rigoristic) and preoccupied with sin.

The initial attempts at reform produced two schools of thought. Morality was effectively reduced to one principle, that of calculating the consequences of an action and opting for the greater proportion of good in any human action. All actions were understood to be essentially determined by their circumstances or particular situation and were assumed to be by nature ambiguous; none was seen to be intrinsically either good or bad. What mattered was that the proportion of foreseeable good effects should outweigh the evil effects. The other school recognized a multiplicity of principles governing any action, while maintaining that some actions (adultery, perjury, murder) were always to be avoided as they were intrinsically wrong, irrespective of the circumstances. Both of these schools, it is now more and more recognized, were still operating from a legalist mental framework, one tending to laxity, the other to rigorism, one dissenting from traditional Catholic teaching, the other defending it. Both have, under the influence of the contemporary revival of Aristotelian ethics and the moral theology of Thomas Aquinas, given way to a recovery of *virtue* as the context for moral discourse. Virtue is ultimately concerned with happiness and holiness as the goal of human life. It reintegrates both the human passions and divine grace into morality. The *Catechism of the Catholic Church* (1994,

1997), for which Ratzinger was finally responsible, has given official sanction, as it were, to the return to Thomist virtue ethics, while the encyclical *Veritatis Splendor* of Pope John Paul II (1993), into which it is presumed Ratzinger had a significant input, has brought to the earlier debate between these two earlier schools a kind of closure. It defends, among other things, the affirmation that certain actions *are* intrinsically wrong and shows the significance of objective morality for stable political life.

Developments in interreligious dialogue raised other new questions and the need for further clarification. This called for an authoritative response from the Church, which the Congregation, under Ratzinger's direction, provided, though it was understandably not always welcomed. And yet, as mentioned already, Cardinal Ratzinger also continued to lecture and publish articles and books in his capacity as a private theologian, entering into the debate and offering his opinions for critical assessment. This side of him was appreciated only by those who were not deterred by his reputation as conservative or the fact that he was prefect of the CDF. There is treasure here waiting to be discovered by younger theologians.

Many of his more recent theological writings were occasioned by his responsibility for overseeing the Congregation's response to pressing issues such as liberation theology or bioethics. The threat posed by liberation theology in Latin America occasioned two documents from the Congregation, *Libertatis Nuntius* (*Instruction on Certain Aspects of the Theology of Liberation*, 1984) which among other things criticized the revolutionary, neo-Marxist roots of this theology, and *Libertatis Conscientia* (*Instruction on Christian Freedom and Liberation*, 1986) which outlined the basis for an authentic theology of liberation true to Catholic tradition. In bioethics, the Congregation published *Donum Vitae* (Gift of life) in 1987 to answer questions raised by developments in bio-technology dealing with experimentation on human embryos and in vitro fertilization. Other documents prompted Ratzinger to do his own homework in preparation for the meetings of the Biblical Commission and the International Theological Commission, which he chaired and which produced such important documents as those on the interpretation of Scripture, the attitude of the Church to the Jews in the New Testament, and the renewal of moral theology. His reflections on these topics were published in theological journals and are more revealing of his own mind.[46] I would like to single out, by way of example, his article on the philosophical and cultural roots of contemporary developments in biotechnology with respect to creating humans in laboratories.[47] This article goes far beyond the limited scope of *Donum Vitae*, which, as already mentioned, is the Church's

---

[46] See, for example, Cardinal Ratzinger's address to the prestigious Westphalian Academy of Sciences (*Westfälische Akademie der Wissenschaften, Geisteswissenschaften: Vorträge* G279, Opladen, 1986). This is a detailed analysis of one of the foundational texts of liberation theology, Gutierrez's *Theology of Liberation*, and probably functioned as part of his homework in preparation for the two *Instructions on Liberation Theology* issued by the CDF in 1984 and 1986. Similarly, his publications on the relationship between Christianity and Judaism, such as *Many Religions–One Covenant* (San Francisco: Ignatius Press, 1999), were probably part of his own study of the question in preparation for the impressive document issued by the Pontifical Biblical Commission *The Jewish People and Their Sacred Scripture in the Christian Bible* (2002), under his chairmanship. See also the text of his address to a historic meeting of rabbis and Church leaders in Jerusalem, 1994 (cf. *Inside the Vatican*, May 2005, 42–44). On his preparatory work on *Dominus Iesus*, see below.

[47] "Man between Reproduction and Creation: Theological Questions on the Origins of Human Life", *Communio* 16 (1989): 197–211. This is an extraordinary article on contemporary developments in biotechnology, outlining the philosophical and theological background in European cultural history (going back as far as the Kabbalah) that is at the root of these revolutionary developments. The article was originally an address given to the University of Bologna, April 30, 1988, and seems to have been part of his reflections on,

response to artificial human reproduction, perhaps one of the most important documents issued by the CDF.

Placed at the center of the universal Church, Cardinal Ratzinger had a unique view of world events that affected his personal theology and found expression in his many writings of this period about what I call his theology of politics. Of particular importance were the political developments in Europe before and after the fall of the Berlin Wall, developments about which he commented fearlessly and, indeed, prophetically. I will take a closer look at his "theology of politics" later in this chapter. In this later period, pastoral concerns tended to dominate his theological writings, very often sparked by the various crises affecting the worldwide Church that called for an authoritative response from the Congregation for the Doctrine of the Faith. As already mentioned, questions treated included liberation theology, developments in biotechnology, and, most recently, the relationship between Christianity and the other world religions, which, incidentally, was one of the topics he had dealt with in his early formative period as an academic theologian. His mature reflections on this last topic are to be found in *Truth and Tolerance*.[48]

Space does not permit us to outline Ratzinger's theological evaluation of the other world religions and their relationship to Christianity. What follows is but the tip of an iceberg. Central to his thought is the fact that religions are not static entities but, like the culture they form and express, are dynamic, ever-changing phenomena. According to Ratzinger, a shared cult, religion, or worship is at the core of

or in preparation for, *Donum Vitae* (the *Instruction on Respect for Human Life in Its Origin and on the Dignity of Procreation*, February 22, 1987).

[48] *Glaube—Wahrheit—Toleranz* (Freiburg im Breisgau: Herder, 2003); English trans. by Henry Taylor (San Francisco: Ignatius Press, 2004).

every ancient culture. This communal cult is rooted in some primordial experience of the ground of all being, an experience that in turn defines the inner character of each culture. But cultures also exist in history and so are subject to change (in the sense both of enrichment and of decay), depending on whether they are open or closed to the universality of truth. Further, cultures interact. "Each particular culture not only lives out its own experience of God, the world, and man, but on its path it necessarily encounters other cultural agencies and has to react to their quite different experiences. This results, depending always on the degree to which the cultural agent may be closed or open, inwardly narrow or broad in outlook, in that culture's own perceptions and values being deepened and purified. . . . A process of this kind can in fact lead to a breaking open of the silent alienation of man from the truth and from himself that exists within that culture"[49]—when his conscience is stirred by an encounter with the truth of human existence. I shall return to this topic in chapter five.

Christian faith results from God's self-communication of himself to mankind in Christ, who is the Way, the Truth, and the Life (Jn 14:6). When the revealed truth of Christianity encounters the search for truth in other religions and cultures, the result can be a mutual enrichment, when the partial or still somewhat obscure truths in the other religions, in particular their own (self-critical) wisdom traditions, find their fulfillment in Christ. This is so because of a conviction that is central to all wisdom traditions but has been denied in the modern world, namely, "the conviction that man's Being contains an imperative; the conviction that he does not himself *invent* morality on the basis of calculations of expediency but rather *finds* it

[49] *TT* 63.

already present in things".[50] As a result, all the great religious and wisdom traditions of mankind flow like tributaries into the great Christian vision of reality, as has been the case since the dawn of salvation history. "The ethical vision of the Christian faith is not in fact something specific to Christianity but is the synthesis of the great ethical intuitions of mankind from a new center that holds them together."[51]

8. Major interviews

It was during his time as prefect of the CDF that Cardinal Ratzinger gave three renowned interviews to journalists, which gave the public a taste of his theology—though they also involved him in further public controversy. All three interviews were given over a short period of time; the second and third took place over two weekends, when the Cardinal and the journalist repaired to a Benedictine monastery outside Rome and spent the whole weekend in conversation. The first interview was with the Italian journalist Vittorio Messori. It was held in the seminary in Brixen, South Tyrol, and was published as *The Ratzinger Report: An Exclusive Interview on the State of the Church*, which dealt primarily with internal Church

[50] TPE 28–29; there Ratzinger takes up and develops the insights of C. S. Lewis, *The Abolition of Man* (London: Oxford University Press, 1943).

[51] TPE 37; with Heinz Schürmann and Hans Urs von Balthasar, *Principles of Christian Morality* [= *PCM*], trans. Graham Harrison (San Francisco: Ignatius Press, 1986), pp. 43–66. In stressing what is common to the wisdom traditions of mankind, Ratzinger may have left himself open to the criticism that he fails to give sufficient attention to what is specifically Christian—that newness which is our life in Christ; cf. Servais Pinckaers, O.P., *The Sources of Christian Ethics*, trans. from the 3rd ed. by Sister Mary Thomas Noble, O.P., (Washington, D.C.: Catholic University of America Press, 1995).

issues.[52] For the younger generation in particular, who were growing dissatisfied with the theology they were getting in seminaries and (in particular) at the university level, it was an eye-opener and the occasion for their liberation as believers.

The second interview was given to Peter Seewald, at the time a lapsed Catholic and a highly respected journalist with the left-wing German daily *Die Süddeutsche Zeitung.* It was published as *Salt of the Earth: The Church at the End of the Millennium* and covers a much broader range of issues, including his own biography and his views on the state of a world about to enter the twenty-first century.[53] It has inspired many and given particular encouragement to the older generation, who remained faithful despite the candy-floss theology they were being offered at the time, which they knew in their heart of hearts could not answer the deeper questions of the human spirit. I refer here to the tendency of theologians to interpret the faith in the light of contemporary trends rather than interpreting contemporary trends in the light of the faith. The at times demanding nature of Christian faith and morals tends to be watered down to make them seem more palatable to a more permissive generation. They are sweet-tasting but lack any real substance. Ratzinger, by way of contrast, has held firm to the intellectually and morally challenging truths of faith and has the ability to throw new light on them within the contemporary cultural context in such a way that old truths

---

[52] Originally published in Italian: *Rapporto Sulla Fede* (Milan: Edizioni Paoline, 1985); English trans. [= *RR*] by Salvator Attanasio and Graham Harrison (San Francisco: Ignatius Press, 1985).

[53] Originally appeared in German: *Salz der Erde: Christentum und katholische Kirche an der Jahrtausendwende* (Stuttgart: Deutsche Verlags-Anstalt, 1996). English trans. by Adrian Walker (San Francisco: Ignatius Press, 1997).

make new sense. For example, when dealing with creation, Ratzinger stresses the truth that at the origin of all reality is loving intelligence (the Word), not irrational blind chance. The effect of reading his theology has for many been truly liberating.

The same journalist, who in the meantime had returned to the Church, conducted a third interview, which was more strictly theological in nature. The result was a kind of popular *Summa* (or systematic treatment) of Ratzinger's theology entitled *God and the World*.[54] It is, in effect, a commentary on the content of our faith. Also of note are two books Ratzinger wrote toward the end of his time as prefect: his autobiography, *Milestones: Memoirs 1927–77*,[55] and, three years later, *The Spirit of the Liturgy*,[56] perhaps the most important of his works in this later period. It was written during a vacation in Regensburg, and Ratzinger hoped that his theology of the liturgy would give rise to a renewal similar to the important liturgical-renewal movement prompted by a book with a similar title published by Romano Guardini in 1918.

9. Moral theology and the theology of political life

Ratzinger's reflections on morality belong primarily to his middle period (see, for example, *Principles of Christian Morality*,[57]

---

[54] Published in German: *Gott und die Welt: Glauben und Leben in unserer Zeit* (Stuttgart and Munich: Deutsche Verlags-Anstalt, 2000); English trans. by Henry Taylor (San Francisco: Ignatius Press, 2002).

[55] First appeared in Italian: *La mia vita: Ricordi (1927–1977)* (Milan: Edizioni San Paolo, 1997); English trans. by Erasmo Leiva-Merikakis (1998).

[56] *Der Geist der Liturgie: Eine Einführung* (Freiburg im Breisgau: Herder, 2000); English trans. by John Saward (San Francisco: Ignatius Press, 2000).

[57] *Prinzipien Christlicher Moral*, with Heinz Schürmann and Hans Urs von Balthasar (Einsiedeln: Johannes Verlag, 1975); English trans. by Graham Harrison (San Francisco: Ignatius Press, 1986).

while his "theology of politics" [58] can be traced back to his earliest research—his doctoral and postdoctoral theses—and to his first writings as an independent author, such as *The Meaning of Christian Brotherhood*[59] and *Die Einheit der Nationen* (The unity of the nations),[60] both of which are developments of insights first found in his doctoral dissertation. The latter is fascinating, among other things, for its insights into the potential evil of nationalism and its threat to the Church as first perceived by Origen of Alexandria, the third-century founder of speculative theology. Again, it is a pity that it has not been translated. As Archbishop of Munich, his pastoral concerns arising from certain developments in the field of European politics gave rise to his mature theology of politics, early intimations of which can be found, for example, in the twelve sermons published under the title *Christlicher Glaube und Europa* (Christian faith and Europe).[61]

A representative selection of his writings on the theology of politics (including an important essay on liberation theology) is included in the volume entitled *Church, Ecumenism,*

---

[58] The term "theology of politics" is one I coined to contrast with "political theology", a concept that Ratzinger rejects, namely, any theology, such as that of J. B. Metz or the classical forms of liberation theology, that involves the instrumentalization of either the Church or the faith for political purposes or the attribution of sacral or salvific significance to politics. Moreover, Ratzinger used the related term "theology of political life" to describe Augustine's understanding of politics, which he forged in his intense debate in the *City of God* with the "political theology" that characterized the sacral nature of the Roman Empire; cf. Ratzinger, *Einheit der Nationen*, p. 80.

[59] *Die christliche Brüderlichkeit* (Munich: Kösel-Verlag, 1960); English trans. (London: Sheed and Ward, 1966; 2nd ed.: San Francisco: Ignatius Press, 1993).

[60] *Die Einheit der Nationen: Eine Vision der Kirchenväter* (The unity of the nations: A vision of the Fathers of the Church) (Salzburg and Munich: Pustet, 1971; reprinted 2005).

[61] *Christlicher Glaube und Europa: 12 Predigten* (Christian faith and Europe: 12 sermons) (Munich, 1981).

and Politics[62] He describes this collection as "essays in ecclesiology", politics, like ecumenism, being but an aspect of his theology of the Church. His theology of politics combines a critique of modernity (understood as the attempt to create a perfect society by social engineering as justified by one political ideology or another) with an attempt to delineate the contribution of Christianity to a humane society and to modern democracy. Here, conscience—understood as personal moral responsibility—plays a key role, as we will see below. Equally significant is the insight that, according to the New Testament vision, there is no place for a "political theology" (such as liberation theology) and, related to this, that there is no template to be found there for politics (and, accordingly, no justification for political ideologies in the strict sense of the term). Politics is the "art of the possible", the arena of practical reason (involving the exercise of the virtues of prudence and justice), and so of compromise—albeit within moral parameters that are, in principle, non-negotiable, though today the latter are no longer recognized as such, because of the dominance of rationalism and utilitarianism. Also significant for an appreciation of his political thought are the collections of talks published under the titles *A Turning Point for Europe?*[63] and, above all, *Truth, Values, Power: Litmus Tests for a Pluralist Society*, which also contains, among other topics, his most important contribution to moral theology, namely, his understanding of conscience.[64]

---

[62] *Kirche, Ökumene und Politik: Neue Versuche zur Ekklesiologie* (Einsiedeln: Johannes Verlag, 1987); English trans. (Slough, 1988). The English translation is rather poor, and there is even a page missing from the text.

[63] *Wendezeit für Europa?* (Einsiedeln: Johannes Verlag, 1991); English trans. by Brian McNeil, C.R.V. (San Francisco: Ignatius Press, 1994).

[64] *Wahrheit, Werte, Macht: Prüfsteine der pluralistischen Gesellschaft* [= *WWM*] (Freiburg im Breisgau: Herder, 1994). An English translation can be found in *Crisis of Conscience*, ed. J. M. Haas (New York: Crossroad, 1996), pp. 1–20,

In *Values in a Time of Upheaval*,[65] the then Cardinal Ratzinger discussed ways of recovering a moral consensus that is both objective and universal in a world marked by globalization and multiculturalism. In it, he returned again and again to the question of the relationship between faith and reason that had been the subject of his inaugural lecture in Bonn in 1959 as a fledgling theologian. Now the topic emerged as an aspect of the wider and more complex picture of the challenges facing a society today marked by modern terrorism, developments in biotechnology, globalization, and the undermining of the traditional means of orientation within all societies affected by the consequences of the Enlightenment and the very existence of highly influential mass media. Ratzinger argued that faith and reason, revelation and enlightenment, need each other in order to liberate the potential in each to confront, and help overcome, the dangers that threaten mankind today and in the immediate future. In this, as in all his writings, Ratzinger combined scholarship with originality. His analysis of current trends resulted in prognostications for the future, and all is expressed in a language that never fails to stimulate the reader and with a clarity that belies the depth of his singularly original theological reflections rooted in reason and revelation.

10. The first encyclical

Pope Benedict's first encyclical, *Deus Caritas Est* (*God Is Love*), is, in a sense, a masterly synthesis of both his dogmatic

---

and Peter Jennings, ed., *Benedict XVI and Cardinal Newman* (Oxford: Family Publications, 2005), pp. 41–52.

[65] *Werte in Zeiten des Umbruchs*, 2nd ed. (Freiburg im Breisgau: Herder, 2005); English trans. by Brian McNeil, C.R.V. (New York: Crossroad; San Francisco: Ignatius Press, 2006).

theology and his theology of politics. It has all the density of his earlier writings, a density that lends itself not to summary, but to exposition. This document also needs to be unpacked, a task that will remain beyond our scope in this essay. It must suffice to draw attention to some of its main characteristics.

As the Pope intimates in his introduction, the encyclical is intended in the first place to be a reminder of the primacy of love in a world threatened by religious hatred and violence. It is most timely. And yet there is more than that to the letter.

What is love? The first part of the encyclical is devoted to exploring the meaning of the word "love", a much-abused term with a whole range of meanings. Here, the Pope sets out to correct some deeply rooted misunderstandings about the nature of both human and divine love. The second part tackles the practical implications of the primacy of love in a world understandably preoccupied with justice.

The Pope's starting point is the experience of falling in love that is oriented to union in marriage, which the Greeks called *eros* (from which we get the English term "erotic"). This is the experience of an ecstasy that seems divine, but one which, if not purified and disciplined, can become destructive. Without due discipline, this experience can degenerate into the erotic as an end in itself, as promoted by a culture that extols unbridled "sex".

On the other hand, a severely spiritualistic understanding of Christian or divine love emerged in the past century that stressed love as entirely giving and selfless. It was given the Greek term for love found in the New Testament, namely, *agape*. By comparison with *agape*, it was claimed, all human love (now falsely called *eros*) is seen as being essentially selfish: a search for one's own satisfaction or happiness. Its effect

was to banish joy from life—as the German philosopher Nietzsche rightly perceived.[66]

Beginning with a philosophical analysis of the phenomenon of falling in love, Pope Benedict XVI shows how the
inner dynamic of *eros*, though rooted in one's own search
for happiness, is directed to the happiness of the other (one
of the characteristics of *agape*). On the other hand, divine
love (*agape*) is described in Scripture in terms of God's *eros*
for his chosen people and finally for mankind. The Proph-
ets of the Old Testament depict God as a lover who has
been jilted by "the wife of his youth" (Hosea). The New
Testament sees in conjugal love the image of Christ's love
for his Church (Eph 5:23ff.). Therefore, there is no opposition between *eros* and *agape*.

What the Pope demonstrates is that the promise inherent
in human love (*eros*) needs divine love (*agape*) to be fully
realized. Human love already anticipates divine love, while
divine love perfects human love.

How did the false opposition between divine love (*agape*)
and human love (*eros*) come about? It is rooted in a false
opposition between spirit and flesh that deeply marks modern culture—the classic expression of which is found in the
work of modern Lutheran theologians, like that of Swedish
bishop Anders Nygren,[67] though it predates them. The
French philosopher Descartes is often blamed. In fact, it
has older, deeper roots, namely, in Gnosticism, the primal
and perennial heresy that sees a radical, fundamental, black-
and-white opposition between spirit and flesh. Benedict XVI
rejects this negative understanding of *agape* and uncovers
the intrinsic interrelationship between *eros* and *agape*, human

[66] The Pope refers to Nietzsche's book *Jenseits von Gut und Böse*, IV, 168.
[67] Cf. Nygren's *Eros and Agape*, first published in Sweden (*Eros och Agape*,
1930–1936; English trans., S.P.C.K., 1932–1941).

and divine loves. Both are ordered to each other. This reflects the relationship between creation and redemption—all that is good in creation, in particular human love in all its manifestations, is not destroyed by redemption but is perfected and taken up into the sphere of divine love.

It is interesting to note how the Pope returns to insights he has articulated in his earlier writings as a theologian, such as his classic work *Introduction to Christianity*. There, for example, he describes the Cross, not as "the work of expiation that mankind offers to the wrathful God, but as the expression of that foolish love of God's that gives itself away to the point of humiliation in order thus to save man".[68] In the same work we find his attempt to explain the mystery of Christ's Resurrection by taking as his starting point the verse from the Song of Songs, the sublime erotic poem in the Old Testament: "Love is strong as death" (8:6).[69]

The second part of the encyclical deals with some of the practical implications of belief in God who is love. Here, "the encyclical speaks of charity, the service of love given by the Church as a community on behalf of all who suffer in body and soul and are in need of the gift of love".[70] He makes two points. The first is that the Church cannot leave care for the suffering to the many philanthropic organizations founded for this purpose. Secondly, he rejects the thesis that, if we could achieve justice in society, then charity would be superfluous. In sum, he points out that justice, which is so necessary, is not enough. People in need, need

---

[68] *IC* 283.

[69] See especially *IC* 301–4.

[70] The Pope's letter to readers of *Familia Christiana*. An English translation by Matthew Sherry appears as an appendix to *Encyclical Letter God Is Love, Deus Caritas Est* (Libreria Editrice Vaticana and San Francisco: Ignatius Press, 2006), pp. 103–8; here, p. 106.

love. They need love, not as an optional extra, but before everything else.

Outlining the centrality of care for the poor, the sick, and the outcast in Scripture and down through the history of the Church, the Pope calls for the reintegration of charitable activity and social work into the fundamental mission of the Church (which, of course, includes her commitment to promoting justice in this world). The mission of the Church is, in the final analysis, to bring all peoples to the knowledge of God who is Love, who created and redeemed us out of love. By doing so, God set the standard for all moral and political activity: namely, respect for the dignity of the other that leads to active love, especially for those most in need.

In these pages of the encyclical, we find a fine synthesis of his earlier writings on the theology of politics. There he rejects all forms of utopianism, attempts to create a better world through social engineering. Catholic theologians after Vatican II were enthusiastic for what were called issues of peace and justice. They sought to put just structures into place in society, if necessary by revolutionary means. The Pope accepts the need to work for just conditions in society. But he rejects the illusion that man can create a perfect world in the here and now. This, too, is a black-and-white, Gnostic temptation that arises from revulsion against the real world in its murkiness. Seeing nothing but evil in this world (corruption, injustice, oppression), highly idealistic people are tempted to tear down the existing society to create a new and better one—a paradise that usually turns out to be nothing on earth (as we know from Marxist societies).

As a theologian, Ratzinger has appealed all his life for a return to reason (in the sense of reasonableness) in political life. This implies reliance on negotiation, dialogue, and debate within generally accepted moral parameters in order to improve society and promote justice. But it also implies that justice is not enough. Even the most just laws and structures, the best organized attempts to help people in need, will not address the deeper need people have for the helping hand, the friendly face, the presence of the neighbor. I once heard him expressing surprise that, with all the talk of renewal in the Church, vocations to active religious congregations devoted to the sick and the needy had almost dried up. Something has gone seriously wrong.

The whole thrust of the encyclical—and, indeed, of his talks and sermons since his election—is, it seems to me, to help Catholics throughout the world to recover what our true mission is: namely, to experience joy in our own lives and to bring that joy into the rest of the world. When human love is taken up and transformed by divine love, and when our lives are lived in the service of love, then we discover that joy which God intended for us from the beginning of time and which lasts for eternity.[71]

---

[71] See the forthcoming book *An Invitation to Joy: The Theological Vision of Pope Benedict XVI*, by Joseph Murphy, to be published by Ignatius Press, San Francisco, 2007.

Chapter Three

THE ROLE OF CONSCIENCE
IN THEOLOGY

While all his writings are replete with insights into the nature of theology, Joseph Cardinal Ratzinger's responsibilities as Prefect of the Congregation for the Doctrine of the Faith necessitated continuous reflection on the nature and mission of theology, including the role played by the Church's teaching authority.[1] Leaving aside this broader theme, we shall confine ourselves here to a few remarks on his theological method. The following observations are based on his more recent writings in the area of moral theology and the theology of politics, but they apply to his dogmatic theology as well. It is a method that could be summed up in the words of Romano Guardini: "to bring the truth to light".[2]

---

[1] See in particular *The Nature and Mission of Theology: Essays to Orient Theology in Today's Debates*, trans. Adrian Walker (San Francisco: Ignatius Press, 1995). With regard to his earlier reflections, see *CEP* 152–66 and his monumental *PCT*, in particular, pp. 315–93.

[2] Romano Guardini, *Berichte über mein Leben, Autobiographische Aufzeichnungen* (Düsseldorf: Patmos, 1984), p. 109, as quoted in *TPE* 66.

In what was at the time one of his rare autobiographical references,[3] Ratzinger recalled that, when he began his theological studies after the War, what motivated him was the question of the *ratio spei*, the question of the reason for our hope (1 Pet 3:15), which in the Middle Ages was the basis of all theology. That is why he chose fundamental theology as his area of specialization.[4] The question involves two complementary concerns that mark his entire theological endeavor: to penetrate to the very roots of the faith and to comprehend the world into which that faith was uttered and continues to be uttered today. Every subject he tackles provokes him to a radical self-questioning of the faith and its mysteries by one who seeks the light of that truth which is God's self-disclosure. This self-disclosure is historical and so from its origins culturally conditioned; on the other hand, since it is God who discloses himself, his self-disclosure transcends all cultures and has the capacity to transform them. Culture is the sphere of values and collective memory in which we live and move and express our being through language and symbol.[5] Since this is the case, culture is essentially mutable, due to the creativity of the human mind, but also due to the fallibility of memory. Thanks to our freedom to choose what is appearance, not truth, culture can also become alienated from the truth, though never from the entire truth. Culture, like all things human, is ambiguous.

[3] In recent years, such autobiographical notices have become more frequent (as in *SE*), culminating in the publication of his short autobiography, *Milestones: Memoirs 1927–1977* [*MM*].

[4] Cf. *TPE* 61–62.

[5] "Culture is the social form of expression, as it has grown up in history, of those experiences and evaluations that have left their mark on a community and have shaped it" (*TT* 60); Ratzinger clarifies the meaning of this definition, *TT* 60–63.

Our Western culture, shaped not least by modernity, is the ever-present background to Ratzinger's theological project, being both a stimulus and a partner in dialogue, a source of inspiration and an object of critique. Ratzinger is acutely sensitive to any change of mood in the world around him and so capable of assessing the slightest blip in the seismograph recording moral and religious change. This is evidenced in all his writings. It is what gave his opening lectures at the university an excitement, and a popularity, that, as I mentioned above, attracted the most diverse students.[6]

The Enlightenment and its influence, both positive and negative, have long claimed Ratzinger's special attention. The modern world is a product of Western European culture rooted in Christianity; now that product is a threat to Christian faith itself. To distinguish the positive contribution of the Enlightenment from its life-threatening errors is one of Ratzinger's primary tasks, as is his concern to enable that new language forged by the Enlightenment to express the truths of faith, indeed, to highlight aspects of that truth that have not been recognized up to now but which, thanks to the Enlightenment, have now come to the surface.[7] What he said on one occasion about contemporary ecclesiology applies, it seems to me, to theology as a whole: It must be "realized today primarily as an exercise in the self-criticism of the intellectual history of the modern age".[8] The related terms of authority, conscience, truth, and freedom are all

---

[6] See, for example, the opening section of *Introduction to Christianity* or his reflections on the changes caused by the events of 1989 to earlier attitudes vis-à-vis science, religion, and morality in *TPE* 113–20.

[7] See, for example, his collection of essays *Values in a Time of Upheaval*, trans. Brian McNeil, C.R.V. (San Francisco: Ignatius Press, 2006), in particular his contribution to a public debate with Jürgen Habermas, pp. 31–44.

[8] *CEP* 27–28.

part of that intellectual history which Ratzinger in various writings analyzes in the light of the history of theology.

1. *Freedom and authority*

The essay "Freedom and Constraint in the Church"[9] illustrates well Ratzinger's theological methodology; it also provides us with an entry into his understanding of conscience and authority. He first uncovers those historical developments that produced the modern concept of freedom before he turns to Scripture for an insight into a specifically theological understanding of freedom, itself the fusion of Greek reason and biblical faith. The article culminates in his attempt to outline a new synthesis of scriptural insight and the modern concept of freedom that throws light on both, which synthesis indeed, it seems to this writer, exercised a profound influence on the revision of the Code of Canon Law (promulgated in 1983), to which he made a significant contribution.

Ratzinger analyzes the shift in the understanding of freedom brought about by the Enlightenment. The Enlightenment did not simply advocate an emancipation from constraint but rather elaborated new forms of constraint arising from rational insight. Instead of the external authorities of inherited customs, roles in society, or even tradition, man should now subject himself only to the internal authority of rational obligation. Deftly, Ratzinger sketches the two main political developments that the Enlightenment project produced in history: on the one hand, freedom through the

---

[9] "Freiheit und Bindung in der Kirche", in E. Corecco, N. Herzog, and A. Scola, *Les Droits fondamentaux du chrétien dans l'Église et dans la société* (Fribourg, 1981), pp. 37–52, reprinted in *CEP* 182–203; quotations are from the latter.

complex web of institutions that constitute modern democracy and, on the other, freedom through the logic of history as envisaged by Marx and Marxism.

Modern democracy, he maintains, is a fragile structure that depends on values and on an ethos that it cannot create of itself but that are indispensable for its functioning.[10] It is, moreover, a structure that has its own internal weakness and a tendency to concentrate power (and so freedom) in the hands of the few who dominate society, especially through their use of the media. On the other hand, the Marxist vision of a future freedom yet to be brought into existence by submitting to the logic of history ends in a total submission to the Party as the bearer of that "logic". This was compounded by the nihilism of Jean-Paul Sartre, who denied the existence of human nature and posited a state of complete indeterminacy that is hell. In other words, "to be free is to be damned", and salvation is found only in the (Communist) Party.

Ratzinger's own criticism emerges from the analysis itself. His analysis of the modern concepts of freedom leads to a provisional definition of freedom. Of its nature freedom must include constraint and obligation (the negative component) and at the same time must be viewed in positive terms as a form of "self-realization, of realizing one's own essential nature and one's potentialities".[11] This in turn leads to the notion of rights and finally law, as the precondition and content of freedom.

Ratzinger then critically examines how the modern understanding of freedom has influenced various recent move-

---

[10] This is a subject to which he returns several times; see, for example, *CEP* 204ff. and, more recently, *Values in a Time of Upheaval*, in particular chap. 1.

[11] *CEP* 192.

ments within the Church. To begin with, there were diverse attempts in the wake of the Second Vatican Council to import democratic *forms* into the Church, but these floundered both on the nature of the Church's essential (hierarchical)[12] constitution and because they were merely forms devoid of content. Improvised demographic forms are necessarily devoid of the actual complex organization of checks and balances that different democratic systems have devised in the course of history and that, having evolved in their respective cultures, are unique to each. Democratic forms as such are of a secondary, derivative nature. But when the formal aspect of democratic freedom is elevated into a [nonexistent] universal model, a new concept of freedom emerges that goes beyond constitutional forms, namely, liberation *from* all institutions by means of "grass roots democracy". This is found in "congregations" experienced as oases of freedom, where those lost in the anonymity of modern society now feel at home. In such a context, the mystery of Church as the universal sacrament is consequently reduced to the "official" Church, one of the many forms of powerful and, so, alienating institutions that stifle freedom. Despite their positive values, congregations of the like-minded who feel close to each other eventually evaporate into "play-acting" and become void. Dissolution leads, finally, to a search for a more complete freedom than either Church or democracy could ever offer, that of the "Kingdom"—now to be achieved by political means. This devalues man by reducing him to the political sphere, which suffocates what is specific to his nature, namely, his openness to transcendence, thus stifling the actual source of freedom.

---

[12] "Hierarchical" here must be understood in its original Greek sense (*hierosarchê*) of "sacred or holy origin". Cf. *CEP* 128.

What then is freedom? Turning to Scripture, Ratzinger examines the Pauline notions of ἐλευθερία [liberty] and παρρησία [frankness]. The Apostle takes them from the Greek tradition and culture and transforms them in the light of faith—or rather uses them to express and unfold the implications of the faith. The first term is taken from Greek social life: the notion of the free citizen as opposed to the condition of a slave. According to Galatians 4:21– 31, it is the baptized who are now free. "To be free means to be the heir, that is, to be oneself the possessor; freedom is identical to the status of son" [13]—and brings with it the rights and obligations of a son, to fulfill the law of Christ. We are full citizens of the People of God, now that we (as πνευματικοί, Gal 6:1) share Jesus' own status of being and must live in accord with that status, even to the point of crucifixion of the flesh. "Undemanding . . . is something this freedom is not." [14]

Biblical freedom is participation, not just in some social structure, but in Being itself. [15] God is free because he is the totality of Being. Earlier Ratzinger drew attention to the logic of that "education for freedom" which emancipatory groups inside and outside Marxism cultivated. The aim of Marxism was to achieve an "unrestricted God-like freedom that has everything at its disposal". The goal, "being like God", was right, but their image of God was wrong. "Being like God means being like the trinitarian God. This means, therefore, to be like the crucified Christ. The education of love as education of θέωσις is necessarily the education of the cross, which does not

[13] CEP 197.
[14] Cf. CEP 198.
[15] Ibid.

for nothing form the key concept of the Pauline doctrine of freedom." [16]

Frankness or outspokenness (παρρησία) is developed (in the light of 1 Thessalonians 2:1–12) as speaking the truth in a world dominated by appearance (δόξα), even though the speaker, Saint Paul, thereby arouses hostility. It is the courage of the free man, as opposed to the cowardice of the slave, namely, those whose speech is molded by flattery, covetousness, or the thirst for glory and who are thus dominated by the need for publicity, material gain, and public opinion, respectively. These are three forms of enslavement. Each of these motives brings about a diminution, in fact, a destruction of being: "People live for appearances and thus their life becomes a sham." To quote Heinrich Schlier: "Truth and freedom, freedom and truth belong together." [17]

The article concludes by drawing some of the implications of the above for the proposed revision of the Code of Canon Law. The details may be left aside in this context, except to say that his proposed introduction of a moderated version of modern human rights language [18] into the formulation of canon law brings to light much that is unexpected. What is noteworthy is the theological method and basic thrust of the article. As Saint Paul had used the terms of his culture to express the faith, Ratzinger in view of that biblical vision adapts the modern

---

[16] CEP 198–99, amended (the second sentence was omitted from the published translation); this point he develops further on pp. 274–75; see also WWM 48.

[17] CEP 200.

[18] See, for example, Canons 208–31 on the obligations and rights of (1) all the faithful (clerics and lay) and (2) the lay faithful; cf. Vincent Twomey, "The New Code and Lay Ministries", Verbum (1983/1984): 361–75.

understanding of freedom and rights in order to serve the new legal framework that expresses the nature of the Church in the legal language of the modern world. In the course of doing this, he throws new light on the nature of the Church and on that freedom which being a Christian entails.

Ratzinger's main point is that the Church exists to make freedom possible in the most profound sense, that is, to afford the possibility of sharing in the divine being. Consequently the "fundamental organization of the Church's freedom must therefore be to ensure that faith and sacrament, in which this sharing in the divine being is mediated, are accessible without diminution or adulteration. The fundamental right of the Christian is the right to the whole faith." [19] All other rights and obligations lead to or from this basic right. He also highlights the contribution of the Church to freedom in the world, the right to believe and worship being the source of all human rights. More specifically, it was the Church that differentiated faith from the sphere of the State and so made freedom of conscience possible. Conscience—the secret core of one's being where one is face to face with God—is the place of true freedom. "Where Church authority remains fully true to her mission and where conscience becomes pure, the antinomy between freedom and constraint is dissolved." [20]

---

[19] *CEP* 201–2; cf. *NMT* 63, 68–69. See Canon 289, which incorporates this principle.

[20] *Kirche, Ökumene und Politik* (Einsiedeln: Johannes Verlag, 1987), p. 182 [this text and the preceding paragraph, which form the conclusion to the whole chapter, have been omitted from the English translation; instead an unsatisfactory précis is given on *CEP* 203].

2. Conscience and Church authority

But it is precisely within the Church today that the relationship between freedom and constraint gives rise to tension, not least that between the theologian and the teaching authority of the Church. On the broader front, there is also tension between conscience and the pronouncements of the Magisterium, especially on moral issues. Finally there is the question of the role of conscience in the exercise of authority, both ecclesiastical and political. These are not separate themes but are interrelated and are treated as such by Ratzinger in various writings, as we have already seen. Moreover, they cannot be examined in abstraction from the concrete structures of Church and State; thus, for example, any treatment of conscience and authority in the Church must include an examination of the nature of the Church's structure, collegial or primatial, while the nature of political authority must be clarified if we are to understand the role of conscience in politics.

The theologian is not an isolated scholar. His subject is the faith, which he does not construct in the abstract but which he receives in and through the Church. This is what Ratzinger calls the "we" structure of the faith,[21] as experienced in Christian initiation, which is a process of personal transformation and, at the same time, a process of incorporation into the community, "of becoming 'we' that transcends the mere 'I' of the ego". Likewise the "act of theo-logy is as such always an ecclesial act for which a social structure is suitable",[22] the social structure being the Church.

---

[21] On the "we" structure of the faith, see in particular IC 56–61; PCT 15–55; see Christopher Ferguson, The Ecclesial Dimension of Faith as Understood by Joseph Ratzinger (STL thesis, Maynooth, 2003), especially pp. 62–76.
[22] CEP 30; cf. also PCT 15–55; NMT 50–61.

The tension between theology and the Magisterium is often described as the tension between conscience and authority, but perhaps it would be more accurate to describe it as the tension between individual conscience and that conscience which is social by nature, namely, the conscience of those who in God's design are ultimately responsible for the Church and her mission. Both are distinct forms of responsibility; both have truth as their object; both are intrinsically interrelated. Irresolvable tension arises, however, when conscience is understood as pure subjectivity and invested with a false autonomy, while authority is seen as heteronymous, if not ultimately arbitrary.[23] We shall return to these themes, but we will first look at the role of conscience in those who exercise apostolic authority within the Church.

a. Conscience in the exercise of episcopal authority

The specific nature of authority as a particular form of the exercise of personal conscience is a theme that often surfaces in Ratzinger's ecclesiology. Reflecting on the structure and tasks of the synod of bishops, Ratzinger affirms: "Christ governs through conscience, by way of [his followers'] consciences. Christ is able to exercise governance over the Church much more effectively the more open and pure are the consciences of those to whom is entrusted the care of their flocks."[24] Bishops' conferences should not simply aim at making resolutions and producing documents but should work "towards consciences becoming more enlightened and thus on the basis of truth more free. It is only in this way that the true liberation of mankind to which the

[23] Cf. *WWM* 27–39.
[24] *CEP* 60, amended.

Church is summoned can be accomplished."[25] This implicit criticism of the mass of documents issuing from conferences throughout the world despite the high quality of some of these texts—is not a superficial critique of the inevitable bureaucratic tendency endemic to large-scale organizations. Ratzinger's critique, it seems to me, is based on the specific nature of the Church and on her mission to mankind, namely, to bear personal witness to the truth, which alone can make us free.

For this reason, Ratzinger sees the role of bishops' conferences primarily as promoting the reciprocal enlightenment of each bishop's own conscience. This is envisioned as an open, ongoing process, a process that the need to issue resolutions and documents could prematurely halt. "The Council . . . wanted specifically to strengthen the role and responsibility of bishops. . . . [This] new emphasis [however] . . . is in reality restrained or actually risks being smothered by the insertion of bishops into episcopal conferences that are ever more organised, often with burdensome bureaucratic structures."[26] Since episcopal conferences have no theological basis, Ratzinger claims (though others disagree), their "documents have no weight of their own save that of the consent given to them by the individual bishops."[27] What is at issue here is a defense of the very nature of the Church based on a truly episcopal structure of personal witness rather than, for example, an attempt to see the Church universal as a federation of national Churches or collectivities.

The episcopal structure of the Church is part of her divinely constituted, apostolic nature and refers quite specifically to

[25] CEP 59.
[26] RR 59.
[27] RR 60.

the personal responsibility of each bishop both for his own particular Church and for the universal Church, a responsibility he cannot abrogate to any collective body, though he exercises it in communion with his fellow bishops throughout the world. More specifically it "is in governing the particular Church that the bishops share in governing the universal Church, and not otherwise."[28] The diocese is the realization in this particular place and time of the universal Church, and, for this reason, the exercise of the bishop's own responsibility for his Church has universal significance, in particular with regard to his specific responsibility for handing on the apostolic faith. Since conscience is where faith dwells, "both the local and the universal Church are most fully represented by someone who follows his . . . conscience. . . . Hence hearkening to one's conscience contributes more to genuine 'representation' than majority decisions that are often prepared by few and accepted by many more for the sake of peace than out of any deep inner conviction."[29]

The collegial authority of the bishops finds expression in their moral unanimity in faith and morals. It is not simply a matter of majority decisions. "The pattern whereby truths are defined as such is not the majority decision but the recognition becoming generally clear that the guardians of the faith united in sacramental communion jointly recognize a statement as a consequence of this faith they hold."[30] When such unity is manifested, then it is the expression of the faith of the Church, which precisely as universal Church cannot err in matters of faith and morals.

[28] *CEP* 52.
[29] *CEP* 59.
[30] *CEP* 58.

b. Conscience in the exercise of papal authority

In the light of the above, it is clear why Ratzinger can affirm that "collegiality and primacy refer to one another".[31] After describing collegiality as an expression of the "we" structure of the faith, he outlines the inner reason for the papal primacy: faith as a witness for which one is personally responsible.[32] Personal responsibility belongs to the very structure of the Bible. There martyrdom, understood as response to the Cross of Christ, "is nothing other than the final confirmation of this principle of named personal responsibility that cannot be transferred".[33] On the basis of this principle, he develops what he calls the martyrological structure of the primacy. Here he draws on the pioneering research of Martin Trimpe, one of his doctoral students, into the theology of the primacy in the thought of Cardinal Reginald Pole (1500–1558).[34]

Within the historical circumstances of the origin of the Church of England as a national Church, Pole's starting point is the insight that rejection of the primacy of the pope undermines the New Testament distinction between civil and ecclesiastical authority. Secular authority is external power, often coercive. Ecclesiastical power is personal and interior: "the powerless yet powerful point of opposition to secular power".[35] Secular power is national and particular; ecclesiastical power is supranational and universal. Martyrdom is the ultimate opposition of the Church to the universalist

---

[31] CEP 44.

[32] This theme was developed by Pope Benedict XVI in his homily at the Lateran, on taking possession of his cathedral church on May 7, 2005.

[33] CEP 34.

[34] M. Trimpe, Macht aus Gehorsam: Grundmotive der Theologie des päpstlichen Primates im Denken Reginald Poles (1500–1558) (dissertation, Regensburg, 1982).

[35] CEP 40.

claims of the State when it seeks exclusive domination in the religious sphere of life, the sphere par excellence of conscience. Pole thus recovers the original New Testament theology of the primacy (cf. Jn 21:18–19): "The primacy is to be understood first of all as witness to the confession of Christ on the basis of witness given personal warranty in martyrdom as the verification of testimony for him who was crucified and victorious on the cross."[36]

In the second place, the primacy represents the guarantee of the opposition of the one universal Church to every particular secular power that yields to its own inherent totalitarian tendency. It is the theology of the Cross that provides Pole with his insight into the primacy. The Cross is the real locus of the Vicar of Christ:[37] "Standing in the place of Christ is standing in the obedience of the cross and thus the *repraesentatio Christi* in the temporal world, keeping his power present as a counterbalance to the power of the world."[38] The pivotal term here is "obedience": the pope is bound to the will of God—God's Word—for which he is personally responsible.[39] This is what turns the *Sedes* into the Cross. Personal responsibility, which forms the core of the doctrine of the primacy, has its

[36] *CEP* 38.

[37] The title highlights the inner unity between Matthew 16:16–19 and John 21:15–19.

[38] *CEP* 42, translation amended.

[39] "The power that Christ conferred upon Peter and his Successors is, in an absolute sense, a mandate to serve. The power of teaching in the Church involves a commitment to the service of obedience to the faith. The Pope is not an absolute monarch whose thoughts and desires are law. On the contrary: the Pope's ministry is a guarantee of obedience to Christ and to his Word. He must not proclaim his own ideas, but rather constantly bind himself and the Church to obedience to God's Word, in the face of every attempt to adapt it or water it down, and every form of opportunism" (*Homily*, at the Lateran, May 7, 2005).

origin in the theology of the Cross and in Christian humility.

The martyrological structure of the pope's primacy has a twofold significance. On the one hand, the papacy bears the authoritative witness to the truth revealed in Christ, and, on the other hand, it implies a rejection of the totalitarian tendency present in all secular authority, a rejection realized through the very powerlessness of conscience. This latter dimension Ratzinger develops in his theology of politics, as we will see. Here we will take a brief look at another aspect of ecclesiastical authority: its binding force on those who believe. He outlines his thought on this subject within the context of recent ecumenical debates.

c. Conscience vis-à-vis the Church's authoritative decisions

In his discussion of the Church's authoritative reception of the firstfruits of the Anglican-Catholic dialogue (ARCIC) and the debate it caused, Ratzinger rejects a notion of tradition that would limit it to the ancient texts of the first millennium and ignore the dogmatic decisions of the second. This would reduce truth to mere customs, a form of antiquarianism, and disqualify the age-old claim to truth inherent in all authoritative decisions. With what right, Ratzinger asks, could the consciences of those in the resulting Church (in this case the "Latin" Church) be bound by such pronouncements?[40] Church authority, which is rooted in the conscience of those who share the apostolic succession

---

[40] Cf. *CEP* 82; here Ratzinger corrects a misinterpretation of an earlier thesis he had defended to the effect that one should not insist on acceptance of the decisions of the second millennium in order to enter into intercommunion with the Orthodox.

and expressed through their moral unanimity, is binding in conscience on all the faithful everywhere. Accordingly, tradition means above all:

> that the Church, living in the form of the apostolic succession with the Petrine office at its centre, is the place in which the Bible is lived and interpreted in a way that binds. The interpretation forms a historical continuity, setting fixed standards but never itself reaching a final point at which it belongs only to the past. "Revelation" is closed but interpretation which binds is not. There can be no appeal against the ultimate binding force of interpretation. So tradition is essentially marked by the "living voice"—i.e., by the obligatory nature of the teaching of the universal Church.[41]

In a word, the new concept of tradition understood as a custom peculiar to a particular Church risks eliminating the question of truth altogether.

The authoritative interpretation of the Church's faith is of a different nature from the work of theology, whose findings, despite scholarly consensus at any one time, "is of its essence open to revision at any time".[42] Since faith is something durable, the ultimate convictions and decisions of the Church's authority have a definitive character. That they are open to development is clear. But such development of its nature must be in harmony with all previous decisions that themselves provide the source of the Church's unity. "Church unity lives from the unity of fundamental decisions and fundamental convictions."[43] These decisions and convictions are those of the conscience of those who

[41] *CEP* 79–80. Ratzinger here summarizes ideas that he had worked out more fully in his contribution to: K. Rahner and J. Ratzinger, *Offenbarung und Überlieferung* (Freiburg im Breisgau: Herder, 1965).

[42] *CEP* 106.

[43] *CEP* 108.

share in the apostolic succession exercising their personal responsibility for the deposit of faith. They do so within the wider community and thus within the context of contemporary theological reflection and the spiritual experience of the Church at large.[44] Episcopal ministry does not imply a monopoly in the Church. But the decisions of the Magisterium, once taken, are binding *in conscience* on all the faithful and on future generations because they are the decisions taken in conscience by those who share in the apostolic succession, the head of which college is the successor of Saint Peter.

Since unity in the Church is essentially moral unanimity based on truth, ecumenism must be understood precisely in terms of the search for truth. No one can foresee how the various confessions will achieve unity. History teaches that it cannot be imposed from above, as it were, but must be the result of interior preparation. Consequently, all Christian communities must "passionately seek the truth together" without attempting to impose anything that does not come from the Lord and at the same time safeguarding what he has entrusted to us. With Christ at the center of ecumenism, perhaps it is possible, according to Ratzinger, to see in the institutional separation something of the significance for salvation history that Saint Paul saw in the division between Israel and the Gentiles (Rom 11:11).[45]

To treat the various Christian confessions as equally valid traditions would in fact undermine their own claims to

---

[44] Commenting on the way growth and insight into tradition are brought about according to *Dei Verbum* 8, Ratzinger states: "... these three factors belong together: experience without reflection remains blind; study without experience becomes empty; proclamation by the bishops without being rooted in the soil of these two has no effect" (*CEP* 116).

[45] Cf. *CEP* 87.

the truth. If one were to agree to regard them simply as (basically human) traditions, "then one would have cut oneself completely loose from the question of truth, and theology would now be merely a form of diplomacy, of politics." [46] This is Ratzinger's ultimate reason for rejecting the ecumenical propositions of Fries and Rahner: [47] Fries and Rahner had proposed that the leaders of Catholic and Protestant congregations should even now unite into one Church on the basis of the various ecumenical agreements reached so far. This assumed that the faithful would be docile enough to obey their leaders and so the leaders would need not fear the threat of rebellion in the ranks. To which Ratzinger responded: "To skip the question of truth ... by means of a few manoeuvres of ecclesiastical politics [as they proposed] would be completely and totally irresponsible." [48]

What seems to have annoyed Ratzinger—as reflected in the unusually strident tone adopted here—in the proposals of Heinrich Fries and Karl Rahner to hasten the ecumenical progress ("a forced march towards unity" Ratzinger called it) [49] was the concept of hierarchy that underlined them:

[46] *CEP* 98.

[47] H. Fries and K. Rahner, *Einigung der Kirchen—Reale Möglichkeit* (Freiburg im Breisgau: Herder, 1983).

[48] *CEP* 114. In other words, once the question of truth was sidelined, then the leaders of the various Christian denominations could get together to negotiate a formula for eventual unity that would presumably satisfy all parties, though it would necessarily involve compromise, as in all political negotiations, the end result of which being ultimately determined by the ability of the negotiators. This would reduce the Church to a political party entering into coalition with other political parties.

[49] *CEP* 108; this was one of the statements that incurred for him the wrath of his critics; the images used (not the point they express) he was willing to retract, lest the use of such metaphors obstruct dialogue; cf. *CEP* 132–33.

hierarchy as domination, not, as it should be according to its Greek etymology, "divine or holy origin". The leaders of the respective Christian denominations were more or less urged to impose a union on their members, despite significant differences in congregational life, trusting in the docility that could be expected from their adherents. But this implies nothing less than a denial of the essence of the Church: a communion of those who believe, that is, a communion created by moral unanimity rooted in free and personal conviction. The position of Fries and Rahner "reflects [a] misunderstanding of hierarchy springing from the Enlightenment, a misunderstanding which manipulates consciences in an impermissible way and noticeably threatens the internal cohesion of the Catholic Church." [50] According to the Enlightenment, the enlightened ruler, possessing superior reason, issues laws, to which, as the bearer of the superior reason, he simply expects his subjects to submit and so to accept his will as the quasi-divinely willed standard of behavior.

Likewise, Ratzinger rejects the proposal for a council of religions as absurd and extravagant. It is based on a false view of democracy, whereby the enlightened ruler is now replaced by a collective made up of delegates whose majority votes bind consciences. Just as in a genuine democracy certain central things are not subject to majority decision, so too in the Church certain fundamental goods are withdrawn from our vote. More significantly, political representation in parliament is of a radically different nature as compared with the sacramental representation that bishops in council exercise.[51] Bishops in council do not invent

---

[50] *CEP* 128 (English translation amended).
[51] As a result "statements of belief that are 'decided' at a council are not 'decisions' in the usual sense. The moral unanimity that is essential for them

something new but articulate what already exists in the Church and make it publicly binding "as a mark by which the *anima ecclesiastica* can be known".[52]

Commenting on the hefty reaction that his initial criticism of Fries and Rahner produced, Ratzinger welcomed in particular the contribution of Eilert Herms, the Lutheran systematic theologian from Munich, whose merit, he says, was to have brought the question of truth once again to the center of theological reflection. In particular, Herms raised "the fundamental question of the relationship between conscience and authority in the mediation of the Christian faith and thus the legitimization of its claim to truth, which is increasingly showing itself to be the fundamental question for the survival of contemporary Christianity."[53]

Ratzinger's criticism of Herms' interpretation of his own tradition need not concern us here. What is significant is the Lutheran theologian's "radical personalization of the act of faith", which tends to reduce Word and sacrament, and thus the Church and her ministry, to the merely human level. This could result in an opposition between conscience—the privileged locus of faith—and a Church authority that is simply human. The Catholic position, grounded in Scripture, recognizes that God's enlightening and saving action is not limited to personal conscience but is also effective through the Body of Christ. What is communal cannot be deemed to be "merely" human, while the divine action cannot be reduced to the interior illumination of the individual:

---

is for the Church the expression of the fact that here the common faith of the Church is being stated" (*CEP* 129–30).

[52] *CEP* 130.

[53] *CEP* 123–24.

Quite the reverse: divine action is always both divine and human and therefore mediated by another human being (the God-man Jesus Christ and his bodiliness). The effect of his action consists precisely in the fact that what counts in the encounter with Jesus Christ is "I" but "no longer I" (Gal 2:20).... The human being is led out of his or her limited ego and obtains a new ego, a new subjectivity in community with him who suffered for us, ... died and rose again.[54]

These concluding remarks lead us into the heart of Ratzinger's ecclesiology, which is beyond our present scope. However, its essential contours must be sketched in order to understand the significance of his insight into the role of conscience in the exercise of authority. That authority has its origins within the mission of the Church and must be seen in terms of her sacramental structure: God works out his salvation of mankind in history though the agency of free human beings whose personal failure cannot prevent his action from achieving its purpose.[55] This can only be understood ultimately when one has grasped something of the mystery of the Church, which Ratzinger describes as "the occurrence of human history being drawn into the sphere of the divine".[56]

d. The conscience of the theologian and that of the Magisterium

The above concluding remarks also take us back to the subject mentioned briefly at the outset, namely, the mutual

---

[54] CEP 126-27.

[55] Cf. Zur Gemeinschaft gerufen: Kirche heute verstehen (Freiburg im Breisgau: Herder, 1991); English trans., Called to Communion: Understanding the Church Today, trans. Adrian Walker (San Francisco: Ignatius Press, 1996).

[56] CEP 118.

relationship between the theologian and the Magisterium, "between the evidence provided by the individual conscience and the joint evidence of the one faith which we can only receive by sharing in believing".[57] Ratzinger admits that it is a relationship that has not been satisfactorily explained. His own attempt takes as its starting point the nature of theology as such. "Theology is born when the arbitrary judgment of reason encounters a limit, in that we discover something which we have not excogitated ourselves but which has been revealed to us."[58] That encounter with the Word, which always precedes our initiative, we call "conversion", a turning from the "I" to the "no-longer-I"[59] and thus the entrance into the "we" of the Church. In a word, the "Church is not an authority which remains foreign to the scientific character of theology but is rather the ground of theology's existence and the condition that makes it possible."[60] Church here is not limited to the Magisterium but includes the *sensus fidei* of the entire People of God,[61] present perhaps especially in the "simple"[62] faithful (lay and clerical), whose faith and practice the teaching authority has an obligation to defend in the face of irresponsible theological speculation.

Neither can what is binding in the teaching of the Magisterium be limited to what has been declared infallible.[63] Ratzinger rightly rejects such a limiting of authoritative

[57] *CEP* 130.
[58] *NMT* 8. "Theology is pondering what God has said and thought before us" (*NMT* 104).
[59] Cf. *NMT* 50–61.
[60] *NMT* 61.
[61] Cf. *NMT* 104–5.
[62] "Simple" is used here in the New Testament sense of *simplex*; cf. Mt 10:16; Phil 2:15.
[63] Cf. *NMT* 111–13.

teaching to infallible statements as a form of legalism. As a *moral* authority, its teaching evidently lacks mathematical precision and admits of degrees. For these reasons it is itself open to theological investigation, that is, the need for continual clarification both at the level of scholarship and by the Magisterium itself. But no aspect of authoritative tradition can be ignored, much less opposed.

The Church understands herself "as the actual environment of reason in its search for meaning [and so] ... must respect the proper responsibility of reason asking questions within the environment of faith".[64] Scientific theology has its own indispensable role to play in the Church, arising from the "dynamism toward truth and understanding inherent in the faith" and what Ratzinger calls the "dynamism of love, which desires to know the beloved more intimately". The former leads the theologian to pursue a dialogue with every reasonable search for truth; the latter moves predominantly inward, striving to fathom the inner logic and depth of the faith.[65] That either of these scholarly endeavors can lead to conflict is obvious. What is ruled out in principle is any opposition between theology and the Church's teaching authority, much less any notion of a dual magisterium between which the faithful must choose. Theology and the Magisterium have different responsibilities toward the truth,[66] the one to explore, the other to mark the limits of that exploration; the one to prevent

---

[64] *CEP* 163–64.

[65] Cf. *NMT* 104.

[66] "Everyone is free—within the framework of the responsibility of conscience before the truth—to think whatever this responsibility permits him to think or to say. But not everyone is free to assert that what he says represents Catholic theology. Here there is a sort of 'trademark', a historical identity which the Magisterium knows it is called to defend" (*NMT* 8).

the teaching of the Magisterium from turning into an ide-ology,[67] the other to prevent theology from cutting the ground from under its own feet.[68] Misunderstandings can arise and must be resolved. For this, both Christian humil-ity and scholarly docility are essential.

Behind these lies the fundamental conviction of faith that in the beginning was reason (cf. Jn 1:1) and with it truth. Man comes from truth and is capable of truth. His basic attitude to truth is receptive.

> The community of the Church is admittedly necessary as the historical condition for the activity of reason, but the Church does not coincide with the truth. It is not the con-structor of truth but is constructed by it and is the place where it is perceived. Truth therefore remains essentially independent of the Church and the Church is ordered towards it as a means. For this reason there is here a gen-uine "and"—theology *and* the Church's teaching authority as realities ordered to each other.[69]

[67] Ratzinger is acutely aware of the danger of turning theology into a type of party-line "orthodoxy": see *CEP* 164; see also p. 159.

[68] It belongs to the nature of Christian faith "to seek its own reason and in that reason itself, the rationality of the real. But in return it places the task on reason, as far as its search is concerned, to recognize in faith the condi-tion for its own effectiveness to be possible and not to push its absoluteness to the point of dissolving its own foundation, for that would mean confusing itself with the divine reason and thus surrendering the communication with the divine reason from which it lives" (*CEP* 153).

[69] *CEP* 160.

Chapter Four

THE ROLE OF CONSCIENCE IN POLITICS

Already in the above discussion we have on occasion touched on Ratzinger's theology of politics, which is, as it were, the reverse side of his ecclesiology. Papal primacy rests on the primacy of conscience; it implies a rejection of the totalitarian tendency in all secular authority. The State's real though limited authority, since it too is of God (indirectly, through the created order of human nature as essentially communal or political), also binds in conscience to the extent that it is just. Hierarchy, as the authority of direct divine origin, evidently relates to conscience in a way other than the authority of the State does. So, also, the way the two powers exercise their authority differs substantially.

1. Conscience, truth, and the limits of political authority

Foundational for Ratzinger's theology of politics[1] is the distinction between the sphere of faith and that of politics first

---

[1] For an introduction, see V. Twomey, "Zur Theologie des Politischen", in *Joseph Kardinal Ratzinger: Von Wiederauffinden der Mitte: Grundorientierung; Texte aus vier Jahrzehnten*, published by the *Schülerkreis*, ed. Stephan Otto Horn et al. (Freiburg im Breisgau: Herder, 1997; 2nd printing 1998), pp. 219–30.

expressed in the apodictic statement: "Render therefore to Caesar the things that are Caesar's, and to God the things that are God's" (Mt 22:21).[2] This amounted, in effect, to the desacralization of secular authority represented by the Roman emperor and so the liberation of politics from the sphere of the sacral, opening politics up to the sphere of human judgment and decision, the sphere of practical reason or ethics.[3] It implies the separation of State and Church, the former a community of necessity (we are born into it), the latter a community of freedom or conviction (we are baptized into it). It also defines the limits set to political authority: the State's authority does not extend into the sphere of worship and faith, but rather it is defined solely by justice in temporal affairs. Conscience is the only effective barrier to any abrogation of these limits. And so freedom of worship is the basis of all human rights and the ultimate barrier to totalitarianism.[4] The recognition of two separate authorities, Church and State, was the historical precondition for the emergence of freedom as *the* basic value in Western civilization. Since neither authority could claim total allegiance in every sphere of human existence, a space was created where, in the course of time, personal responsibility and conscience could emerge and flourish. This was essentially the unique contribution of the martyrs to the progress of civilization.[5]

---

[2] Cf. *CEP* 161–63; 174, also pp. 171; 202–3; 216–17; again it should be noted that a substantial amount of text has been omitted in the English version before the second to the last line on p. 216, making the translation incomprehensible at this point.

[3] Cf. *CEP* 216–17; see comments on the translation in the previous footnote.

[4] "The right to believe is the real core of human freedom; when this right is lacking the loss of all further rights of freedom follows after with [an] inner logic. At the same time this right is the real gift of freedom that Christian faith has brought into the world" (*CEP* 202).

[5] "The growth of freedom that mankind owes to the martyrs is infinitely greater than that which it could be given by revolutionaries" (*CEP* 174).

Conscience, it could be said in this context, is essentially about limitation, the recognition of those limits that are essential to the preservation of our humanity with its openness to transcendence; these limits we call morality. Every false interpretation of conscience sooner or later reveals itself to be a more or less disguised claim to be unlimited, that is, to be God. In the political sphere it leads ineluctably to anarchy and tyranny.

His political thought brings Ratzinger inevitably to the question of morality and its foundations. Like other contemporary thinkers,[6] he attributes the contemporary denial of objectivity in moral (or ethical) questions to a consequence of the widespread denial of transcendence, namely, the reduction of reason to empirical or quantitative rationality. Relativism also poses the greatest of threats to the body politic. Reducing reason to the world of "facts" and utility results in the annihilation of morality (practical reason) and thus to the abolition of man (to use the title of a well-known essay by C .S. Lewis, which Ratzinger quotes). This can only lead to the exercise of naked power devoid of moral constraint—and so the control by the few of the many. The existential question of our age is, according to Ratzinger, the threat of totalitarianism.[7] And the destruction of conscience is the precondition for totalitarian obedience.[8]

It is not for the Church to wield power in the temporal sense but to awaken man to God and thus to the power of conscience and so, as was mentioned earlier, to keep open

---

[6] See, for example, Eric Voegelin, *The New Science of Politics: An Introduction* (Chicago: University of Chicago Press, 1952), and Václav Havel's collection of essays entitled *Living in Truth*, ed. Jan Vladislav (London: Faber and Faber, 1986), whose writings echo many of the fundamental insights of Ratzinger.

[7] Cf. *CEP* 167.

[8] Cf. *CEP* 165.

the narrow pass between anarchy and tyranny.[9] Central to this is the task of theology, which, according to Ratzinger, is not simply concerned with the interpretation of texts: "it asks about truth itself and it sees man as capable of truth." [10]

The public denial of God leads inevitably to the redivinization of society—the assumed immanence of God in history[11]—and manifests itself in the attempts to create the "perfect society", paradise on earth, and so attempt to change man by changing the structures of society. Social engineering of this kind necessarily denies man his freedom; it also ignores the irredeemable imperfection of the human condition: "The longing for the absolute in history is the enemy of the good in it." [12] Accordingly, the significance of theology for politics would seem to be threefold: it affirms God as the only absolute and (so) relativizes all human structures, including political structures. It also points out that compromise, within the parameters of objective, non-negotiable morality, is of the essence of politics. And, in the face of a materialism that is the inevitable result of atheism, theology finally affirms *reason* as the source of all that is[13] and thus the reality of objective morality as the unmeasured measure of all laws[14] and human behavior. In other

---

[9] Cf. *TPE* 55; cf. *CEP* 254; 263.

[10] *CEP* 154.

[11] Cf. *CEP* 264.

[12] *CEP* 206.

[13] When the Prologue to Saint John's Gospel describes Christ as the Logos, it is expressing "the conviction that in Christian faith what is rational, basic reason itself comes to light and is indeed trying to say that the foundation of being is itself reason and that reason does not represent an accidental by-product from the ocean of the irrational from which everything really came" (*CEP* 152–53; cf. also p. 239).

[14] Cf. Ratzinger, "Eschatology and Utopia" in *CEP* 228, 232, especially 237–40, 243–48. See also *CEP* 228–29, 232.

words, theology, as understood by Ratzinger, takes up the fundamental questions of Greek philosophy, which had first raised the human mind to a new level by asking "the question of truth itself, of being itself".[15]

2. *The relationship between political power and conscience*

But it is faith that awakens conscience. Ratzinger rightly talks about the mystery of conscience, which is essentially powerless yet limits the exercise of power and protects the powerless.[16] He developed his understanding of the political significance of conscience in a lecture he gave on Reinhold Schneider's novel about Bartholomé de Las Casas.[17] The subject of that novel, he claims, is the relationship between power and conscience. Three personages represent conscience, the anonymous fragile girl from the Lucayos, Las Casas himself, and Emperor Charles V. The Lucayan girl is the purest form that conscience can take: the suffering of the innocent, who even suffers for her persecutors. Las Casas represents the prophetic conscience awakened by a text of Scripture; he became the guilty conscience of the powerful and the defender of the sovereignty of the law that transcends man and is found ultimately in one's own conscience. It is the interior law (*nomos*), the source of all laws.[18] Charles V represents the conscience of one to whom

[15] *CEP* 154.

[16] Cf. *CEP* 172.

[17] Cf. "Conscience in Its Age", in *CEP* 165–80, originally appeared in German in *Internationale katholische Zeitschrift Communio* 1 (1972): 432–42; also in *Reinhold Schneider Gesellschaft e.V.*, Heft 4, July 1972, 13–19. Schneider's novel is entitled *Las Casas vor Karl V. Szenen aus der Konquistadorenzeit*. On Reinhold Schneider, see *Reinhold Schneider und die Politik: Zwischen Macht und Gewissen*, 2nd ed. (Ulm-Kislegg: Gerhard Hess Verlag, 1942), pp. 4, 136–43.

[18] Cf. in this connection: *CEP* 228–29.

power is entrusted to be exercised with responsibility. He bears power as a burden, a suffering, and lives under the restraint of power that his own conscience imposes.

Ratzinger is naturally aware of the difficulty in trying to articulate precisely what conscience is and of the inherent dangers in appealing to conscience when one is simply appealing to convention or trying to justify one's stubborn refusal to be corrected. Something great, like conscience, can be abused when called into play, he warns, though such misuse cannot destroy its intrinsic greatness. Following Schneider, he affirms that conscience amounts to the recognition of man—oneself or others—as God's creatures and so respects the Creator's claim on us. "This defines the limits of any power and at the same time [gives it] its direction. To this extent, insistence on the powerlessness of conscience[19] remains the fundamental precondition and the inmost core of every true restraint on power."[20] In other words, conscience is the recognition of claims that arise from our dignity as creatures of God answerable to him for ourselves and others. Power is limited by these claims, which claims are in turn capable of giving direction to those in authority about how they should use their power. Political, economic, and military power can only be controlled from within, by the conscience of those who exercise political authority and who, when they fail, must be resisted by the person of conscience protesting against the exploitation of the powerless. This will inevitably entail suffering, which is the only way, ultimately, that injustice can be overcome.

---

[19] That is, true conscience relies solely on the strength of the truth it grasps—not on any other power, political, economical, or even legal.

[20] *CEP* 170; translation slightly altered.

Whatever the misery caused by the strange hybrid of Christian mission and colonial exploitation that was the Spanish Conquest of Latin America, the sole means of correction was that provided by faith itself, which arouses conscience to struggle and suffer. "The only thing that justifies this faith as truth is that on the basis of its founding principle it may not be a multiplication of power but the summons that awakens the conscience that limits power and protects the powerless. It is here that it has its absoluteness, in the protection of the other as creature." [21]

Impressive though it is, there is something unsatisfactory in the definition of conscience just given. It makes perfect sense in the extreme situation in Latin America described by Reinhold Schneider, where the modern concept of human rights first surfaced, based not on citizenship or baptism but on simply being a creature and so transcending race and religion. From all that was said previously, it is evident that conscience understood as the recognition of the other as creature, the acknowledgment of the Creator's claims on the other and on oneself, though a profound, existential insight into the depths of what Scripture calls "the heart", is not a sufficient description, much less a definition.

In a book of meditations entitled *Der Gott Jesu Christi* (The God of Jesus Christ), Ratzinger concludes his meditation on the Creator God, which echoes many of the themes mentioned above, with the following reflection on conscience:

> Faith in the Creator God is at the same time faith in the God of conscience. Because he is Creator, for this reason he is close to each one of us in [our] conscience. The entirely personal content of the confession of faith in creation is

[21] *CEP* 172.

demonstrated in belief in conscience. Conscience is above the law: it distinguishes between the law that is just and the law that is unjust. Conscience signifies the primacy of the truth. That, however, means: it is not a principle of arbitrariness, but rather an expression of faith in the secret co-knowing of man with the truth. In [our] conscience, we are co-knowers of the truth, and thus conscience challenges us at the same time to be ever more in search of the truth.[22]

Before we turn to consider Ratzinger's own attempt to describe the nature of conscience more precisely, let us look at a classic expression of his theology of politics, where he turns his attention to the existential situation in which Western democracy finds itself: "A Christian Orientation in a Pluralist Democracy?"[23] The question mark is important.

3. Democracy, the Church, and conscience

Ratzinger is acutely aware that modern democracy cannot stand on its own but needs other moral resources to maintain itself. He looks at the pluralist democracies of Europe and notes their many weaknesses, particularly their tendency to expect too much from society. This attempt to create a new world that will finally, definitively be a better world is the greatest threat to democracy itself. Behind this threat is the persistence of the Gnostic dream of establishing the Kingdom of God *within history* once and for all. "The longing for the absolute in history is the enemy of

---

[22] J. Ratzinger, *Der Gott Jesu Christi: Betrachtungen über den Dreieinigen Gott* (Munich: Kösel, 1976), pp. 39–40. I am grateful to Joseph Murphy for drawing my attention to this text.

[23] CEP 204–20; on p. 216 almost two paragraphs have been omitted from the translation.

the good within it."[24] The myth of the creation of a perfect society here on earth engenders revulsion against the imperfections of existing society and can engender anarchy in the irrational hope that once the present corrupt society has been destroyed, a new and better world will emerge. This is the seedbed of political terrorism.

a. Democracy under threat

Ratzinger distinguishes three interrelated aspects of the threat to democracy. The first is the assumption that perfect justice can be achieved simply by changing the economic, social, and legal *structures* of society. A "perfect society" of the future would supposedly be a society liberated from all kinds of exploitation and injustice by new structures (in other words, social engineering). In fact, it would "free" the members of society from the continual moral effort needed to achieve justice in society. Such a "liberation" would in effect amount to nothing less than the abdication of personal responsibility and personal freedom. It presupposes perfect tyranny. But "neither reason nor faith ever promises us that there will ever be a perfect world."[25] To toy with the idea is to encourage a false "enthusiasm bent on anarchy".[26] Today's pluralist democracy, for all its imperfections, allows a certain measure of justice to be achieved within clear limits, and some improvement is always possible. For democracy to continue to develop, it is urgently necessary to acquire again "the courage to accept imperfection"—and to learn to appreciate that human affairs are constantly endangered

[24] *CEP* 206.
[25] *CEP* 208.
[26] Ibid.

and so call for constant vigilance. Any moral appeal based on the promise of a perfect society in the future is in fact profoundly immoral—it encourages a *flight from morality*,[27] from free, human, prudential decisions, toward some form of utopia.

The attempt to make morality with all its shortcomings superfluous by promoting the creation of a perfect society has another root. This is the one-sided concept of reason characteristic of modernity, what Václav Havel likewise calls impersonal reason. Anything that cannot be quantified, calculated, or verified by "scientific experimentation" is regarded as irrational, illogical. This amounts to the abolition of morality as such. Human decision-making is reduced to an attempt to balance the foreseen advantages or disadvantages of a proposed course of action. Morality becomes personal preference—and so "law has the ground cut from under its feet." [28] If there is no such thing as objective morality, then the law can no longer be conceived as giving legal protection to that which is intrinsically good and forbidding what is intrinsically wrong; it becomes a mere means for preventing opposing interests from clashing with one another. When moral reason is conceived as basically irrational—merely a matter of subjective preference—law can no longer be referred to as a fundamental image of justice but becomes the mirror of the predominant view of the experts or, more frequently, majority opinion. Since views and opinions in society are subject to constant change—and, indeed, can be profoundly unjust—it is obvious that justice cannot be achieved in this way. Society and the State can only survive if we

[27] Cf. Ibid.
[28] *CEP* 210.

succeed in reestablishing a fundamental moral consensus in society.

The third threat to modern democracy embraces and extends the previous two. If people are convinced that all there is to life is what we experience here and now, discontentment and boredom can only increase, with the result that more and more people will look for some kind of escape in a search for "real life" elsewhere. Escapism and various forms of "dropping out" become endemic. "The loss of transcendence evokes the flight into utopia", Ratzinger states categorically. "I am convinced that the destruction of transcendence is the actual amputation of human beings from which all other sicknesses flow. Robbed of their real greatness they can only find escape in illusory hopes." [29] One such illusory hope is the construction of a perfect society in the future, which Marx claimed could only come about if people first abandoned God.

b. Dangers to democracy posed by Christianity

The modern State is an imperfect society, not only in the sense that its structures will necessarily be as imperfect as its members, but also in the sense that it needs a source outside itself in order to be able to survive and thrive. The question is: What source? Before recommending Christianity, Ratzinger engages in a self-criticism of Christianity as a historical entity and a political force. As a human phenomenon, Christianity (Catholic, Orthodox, Protestant, Anglican), too, is subject to the ambiguity of the human condition. In the course of its history, it, too, has given rise to movements and social tendencies that have unhealthy

[29] CEP 211.

implications for political life and that cannot be ignored. Ratzinger considers three such tendencies.

The first is to misunderstand Christian hope in either purely otherworldly terms or as something to be looked forward to here on earth. The first error encourages Christians to neglect life in society for the sake of the world beyond. The second is the Gnostic temptation to create the Kingdom of God on earth. True Christian hope is the mean between these two extremes. It is the theological virtue that enables Christians to endure injustice patiently and to work unceasingly for justice in this world in anticipation of the Final Judgment in the next.

The second unhappy Christian tendency is the rejection of justification based on human effort ("merit"), which means that human endeavor is considered to be of little consequence for salvation. The resulting notion of holiness based on grace alone, which is granted only to the "saved", permits no accommodation with those who are not "justified" or "saved". This in turn promotes a very black-and-white picture of human society and rules out any compromise, with disastrous results. Since politics is the art of the possible, compromise is essential for political life.

The third tendency is really a danger inherent in the very nature of Christian monotheism, namely, the Christian claim to truth, which has more than once led to political intolerance. There is but one God, who revealed himself in Christ. Consequently, Christianity could not fit into the Roman concept of tolerance based on polytheism. The Romans considered the various cults in the Empire as religious clubs, each free to organize its own private laws and follow its own gods. But Christianity could not accept such a place in society, because it would have reduced Christ to one god among many. Christian belief implied a claim to public recognition comparable to the State's. It also denied the State's claim to absolute obedience. Christianity has from its origins been the adversary of all forms of State totalitarianism. But the claim to ultimate truth can result—and has in the past resulted—in political intolerance, once the Church herself became a political force. Theocracy is an inherent danger, meaning not simply rule by priests (that has been extremely rare) but rather the attempt to rule society according to explicit religious beliefs, as today in the case of Islam. Theocracy is thus inimical to the basic understanding of political life found in the New Testament. But it is an ever-present temptation.

c. The central question

The central question, as Ratzinger sees it, is: "How can Christianity become a positive force for the political world without [itself] becoming turned into a political instrument and without on the other hand grabbing the political world for itself?"[30] His answer again is threefold.

First, from its origins in the life of Christ, Christianity on the whole has refused to see itself as a political entity. One of the three temptations faced by Christ at the beginning of his public ministry that of transforming the Kingdom of God into a political program. "My kingdom is not of this world", Jesus affirmed. "Give to Caesar what is Caesar's and to God what is God's." Caesar represents the State, the realm of political life, which is the realm of practical reason and human responsibility. According to Ratzinger, the New Testament recognizes an *ethos* or sphere of political responsibility but rejects a *political theology*, that is,

---

[30] *CEP* 216.

a political program to change the world on the basis of revelation. Thus all attempts to establish a perfect society (the Kingdom of God on earth) are rejected by the New Testament. The New Testament rejection of justification by one's own effort is likewise a rejection of political theology, which would claim that a perfect society based on justice could be established by human effort alone. Perfect justice is, rather, the work of God in the hearts of those who respond to his love (grace). Justice in society cannot be achieved simply by changing the structures of society but is rather the temporary result of continued imperfect efforts on the part of those who make up society. To accept this is to acknowledge the imperfection that characterizes our human condition and to accept the need to persevere in one's own moral effort. Such endurance in trying to do what is right, to find the right solution to the practical difficulties that arise from daily life in common, is made possible by grace and the promise of everlasting life and ultimate victory in Christ. "The courage to be reasonable, which is the courage to be imperfect, needs the Christian promise [that is, the theological virtue of hope] to hold its own ground, to persevere." [31]

Second, Christian faith awakens conscience and thus provides a necessary foundation for the ethos of society. Faith gives content and direction to practical reason. It provides the necessary co-ordinates for practical decision-making. The core of the crisis of modern civilization is the implosion of the profound moral consensus that once marked all the great traditions of humanity, despite their superficial differences.

---

[31] *Kirche, Ökumene und Politik: Neue Versuche zur Ekklesiologie* (Einsiedeln: Johannes Verlag, 1987) [= CEP], p. 194 in the German edition (missing from the English translation).

If there is nothing intrinsically right or wrong, conscience can be relegated to the private sphere and law can no longer be regulated by morality. Accordingly, the most urgent task for modern society is to recover the meaning of morality and its centrality for society, which is constantly in need of inner renewal. A State can only survive and flourish to the extent that the greater number of its citizens are themselves trying to do what is right and avoid what is wrong—insofar as they are truly trying to act in accordance with their conscience and striving to become virtuous. Thus genuine moral formation, by which one learns how to exercise one's freedom, is essential for the possibility of establishing justice, peace, and order in society. Moreover, it is important to remember that the basic morals of modern Western society are the morals of Christianity, with its roots in Judaism and classical Greek thought. It is the residue of these that, filtered through the Enlightenment, gives modern democracy its internal ethical framework. When the Christian foundations are removed entirely, nothing holds together any more. Reason needs revelation if it is to remain reasonable—if it is to recognize those limits that define us as human beings.

The third and final point touches on a most sensitive aspect of the interconnection between Christianity and modern pluralist democracy. Today few will deny Christianity the right to develop its values and way of life alongside other social groups. But this would confine Christianity to the private sphere, just one value system among other, equally valid ones. Not only does this contradict the Christian claim to truth and universal validity, it robs Christianity of its real value to the State, which is that it represents the truth that transcends the State and for that very reason enables the State to function as a human society guided by the conscience of its members. Thus we have the dilemma. If the Church gives up her claim to universal truth and transcendence, she is unable to give to the State what it needs: the strength of perseverance in the search for what is good and just as well as the source of its ultimate values. On the other hand, if the State embraces the Christian claim to truth, it can no longer remain pluralist, with the danger that the State would lose its own specific identity and autonomy. Achieving a balance between the two sides of this dilemma is the prerequisite for the freedom of the Church and the freedom of the State. Whenever the balance is upset and one side dominates the other, both Church and State suffer the consequences. Christianity is the soil from which the modern democratic State cannot be uprooted without decomposing. The State, Ratzinger insists, must accept that there is a stock of truth, which is not subject to a consensus but rather precedes every consensus and makes it possible for society to govern itself.

The State ought to show its indebtedness in various ways, including the recognition of the validity of the public symbols of Christianity—public feast days, church buildings and public processions, the crucifix in schools, and so on. Yet, such public recognition can only be expected, adds Ratzinger, when Christians themselves are convinced of their faith's indispensability, because they are convinced of its ultimate truth. Conscience, the created echo of truth in our hearts, has recognized the divine source of that echo and submitted to it in the obedience of faith. But this is to anticipate the next chapter.

Chapter Five

WHAT IS CONSCIENCE?

*Stillness means to develop the inner senses, the sense of con-
science, the sense for the eternal in us, the ability to hear God.*

—*Joseph Cardinal Ratzinger, Der Segen der Weihnacht*

In a recent publication[1] containing three short essays, Ratzinger directly addresses the question of the meaning of con
science as such. We can leave aside the first and last essays,
which develop many of the points mentioned above, in particular the significance of conscience, and with it objective
morality, for today's political life, marked as it is by relativism. The core of the book would seem to be the second
essay, entitled: "Conscience and Truth". In it, it seems to
me, he cuts the Gordian knot at the heart of that contemporary crisis, in the Church and in the world, which could
be summed up as the triumph of subjectivity, the denial of
man's capacity for truth and, so, for God. It is a crisis that,
unresolved, renders society incapable of justice or the defense
of the weakest (in the womb or on the edge of the tomb),

[1] *WWM.* (Quotations below have been translated by this writer.) For an
earlier sketch of the insight articulated here, see Joseph Ratzinger, "The
Church's Teaching Authority—Faith—Morals", in *PCM* 64–65, 70–73.

that engenders nihilism (symbolized by drugs, terrorism, and suicide), and that has dried up the Church's missionary zeal at a time when the world never needed the healing word of truth more urgently.

1. The primal level of conscience

What Ratzinger achieves in this essay is the recovery of what might be described as the ontological level of conscience, which in the Middle Ages was known as *synderesis*, a term taken from Stoicism, as distinct from *conscientia*, the level of judgment, that is, conscience in the narrow sense of the term, which is what most people mean when they use the term, even when in fact they may wish to refer to the deeper level. To describe the ontological level of conscience, Ratzinger prefers the more clearly defined Platonic term *anamnesis* (recollection, primal memory) to the Stoic term. It is a term, moreover, that is close to biblical thought, such as when Saint Paul describes in Romans 2:14–15, the law that is written into our hearts. This ontological level of conscience was central to tradition from Saint Basil the Great and Saint Augustine to the mediaeval mystics and the Schoolmen such as Saint Thomas Aquinas. It was first discovered by Socrates, whom Ratzinger regards as a kind of prophet of Jesus Christ; it is central to the thought of Cardinal Newman.[2] But in modern post-Scholastic theology, it was effectively forgotten,[3] with the consequent shriveling of conscience to the second level, that of judgment.

[2] Ratzinger does not mention it explicitly, but evidently he refers here in the first place to Newman's *An Essay in Aid of a Grammer of Assent* (1870).

[3] The great exception here, as usual, was Josef Pieper: cf. his *Traktat über die Klugheit* (Munich: Kösel, 1949), pp. 23–36 (in the 6th printing in 1960); English trans. by Richard and Clara Winston and others, *The Four Cardinal*

Neglect of attention to the ontological level of conscience led eventually to two apparently contradictory, but in fact closely related, perversions of the notion of conscience prevalent in our day, a false notion of what an "erroneous conscience" entails[4] and the related notion of an "infallible conscience". "Erroneous conscience" has come to mean in effect that it does not matter what one does provided that one is sincerely convinced that it is right. "Infallible conscience" affirms that conscience cannot err, that what you think is right is in fact right. Conscience is reduced to an "excuse mechanism".[5] Both notions receive their persuasiveness, if not their inspiration, from the prevailing relativism,[6] the end product of the Enlightenment project that was built on the autonomy of the subject and the absolute claims of reason—having reduced reason to empirical or quantitative rationality—and is now floundering in uncritical conformity to convention.[7]

Both misunderstandings of what conscience is reflect that all-pervasive subjectivity which reduces morality to personal

---

Virtues (New York: Harcourt, Brace and World, 1965), pp. 10–17 ; see also *Die Wirklichkeit und das Gute* (Munich: Kösel, 1949); Pieper's term for the ontological level of conscience is *das Ur-Gewissen* (primal conscience).

[4] Here Ratzinger draws attention to the research of J. G. Belmans, "Le Paradoxe de la conscience erronée d'Abélard à Karl Rahner", in *Revue Thomiste* 90 (1990): 570–86, which demonstrates that, with the appearance of *La Philosophie morale de Saint Thomas d'Aquin* by A. D. Sertillanges (Paris: F. Alcan, 1916), a falsification of Aquinas' teaching on conscience began that has been widely influential.

[5] *WWM* 39.

[6] See Peter Funk, "Die Kunst des Steuermanns: Aristoteles' Beitrag zu einer theologischen Lehre vom Gewissen", in K. Arntz and P. Schallenberg, eds., *Ethik zwischen Anspruch und Zuspruch* (Fribourg: Universitätsverlag; Freiburg im Breisgau: Herder, 1996), pp. 284–300, for some useful information about the historical origins of the two notions.

[7] Cf. *CEP* 153–54, 231–32; *TPE* 31–35; *WWM* 65–73.

preference, something ultimately irrational. "In such a 'relativistic' context," Ratzinger mentions in an aside,

> teleological or consequentialist ethics [still the predominant school of thought in Catholic moral theology] becomes in the final analysis nihilistic, even when it does not discern it. And when in such a world view one mentions "conscience", the description for it is—more profoundly considered—that there is no such thing as conscience as such, namely co-knowing with truth. Each one determines his own criteria, and in the general relativity no one can be of assistance to the other, much less make regulations for him." [8]

What, then, is the ontological level of conscience? It is "the window that opens up to man the view of the truth common to us all that establishes and sustains us and so makes community of decision and responsibility possible due to the common ground of perception".[9] Pure subjectivity, on the other hand, disposes of the obligation to search for the truth and removes any doubt about generally accepted attitudes. It suffices to be convinced about one's own views and adjust to the views of others: the more superficial one's views, the better. But a firmly subjective conviction untouched by guilt is in fact a symptom of a sickness of the soul.[10] The inability to experience guilt is the sin of the Pharisees.

Interpreting Romans 2:1–16, where Paul undermines the theory of salvation through lack of knowledge of the truth (in other words, due to an erroneous conscience), Ratzinger says:

[8] *WWM* 46.
[9] *WWM* 32.
[10] Ratzinger (*WWM* 34–35) refers to the psychologist A. Görres, "Schuld und Schuldgefühl", in *Internationale katholische Zeitschrift Communio* 13 (1984): 434.

There is in man the presence of truth, which cannot be disallowed—that truth of the Creator which in salvific-historical revelation has also become written down. Man can see the truth of God as a result of being created. Not to see it is guilt. It is not seen if and because it is not willed. This "no" of the will that prevents knowledge is guilt. Then the fact that the signal-lamp does not light up is a consequence of an intentional looking away from that which we do not want to see.[11]

According to Newman, who rejected the liberal notion of the subject as a self-sufficient criterion over against the demands of authority in a world devoid of truth, conscience means, in Ratzinger's words, "rather the audible and imperious presence of the voice of truth in the subject himself; conscience is the cancellation of pure subjectivity in the contact made between the interiority of man and the truth that comes from God."[12]

The first, as it were, ontological level of conscience, then, consists in the fact "that something like a *primal memory* [*eine Urerinnerung*] *of the good* and *of the true* (both are identical) is implanted in us; that there is an inner tendency of being in man made in the likeness of God toward that which is in conformity with God. . . . This anamnesis of the origin, which results from that constitution of our being which is in conformity with God, is not a conceptual, articulated knowledge, a treasury of recallable contents. It is, as it were, an interior sense, a capacity of re-cognition, so that the person who is thereby addressed, if he is not interiorly opaque, recognizes the echo of it in

[11] *WWM* 37.
[12] *WWM* 43.

himself." [13] Saint Augustine formulated it more simply as the sense for the good that is imprinted in us. [14] However, this sense needs, as it were, help from without in order to become itself; what is outside it performs a maieutic function to bring its openness for truth to fulfillment. What is "outside" is the authority of the Church [15]—but also presumably includes any genuine moral authority, though Ratzinger does not mention this. With regard to the Church there is yet another dimension to be mentioned that goes beyond the radius of creation: the anamnesis of the new "we" that has been granted to us through our sacramental incorporation into Christ. Saint John appeals to this Christian memory, which is always learning but which on the basis of its own sacramental identity can distinguish between what is the unfolding of Christian memory and what is its falsification (cf. 1 Jn 2:20). [16]

[13] *WWM* 51–52. "To a certain extent I am a Platonist. I think that a kind of memory, of recollection of God, is, as it were, etched in man, though it needs to be awakened. Man doesn't simply know what he is supposed to know, nor is he simply there, but is a man, a being on the way" (*SE* 41).

[14] *WWM* 51–52. "To a certain extent I am a Platonist. I think that a kind of memory, of recollection of God, is, as it were, etched in man, though it needs to be awakened. Man doesn't simply know what he is supposed to know, nor is he simply there, but is a man, a being on the way" (*SE* 41). Cf. *WWM* 51, 53. See Saint Augustine, *De Trinitate* VIII, 3 (PL 42, 949). I am grateful to Msgr. Joseph Murphy for this reference.

[15] Cf. *WWM* 53–54. See also the address of Pope Benedict XVI to the participants at the international conference on the human genome (November 19, 2005): "I would like to point out that today, especially in the area of breakthroughs in medical science, the Church is being given a further possibility of carrying out the precious task of enlightening consciences, in order to ensure that every new scientific discovery will serve the integral good of the person, with constant respect for his or her dignity" (Zenit).

[16] *WWM* 54–55.

2. Conscience as judgment

The second level of conscience comes into play in the act of judgment in a particular situation, which of its nature is always unique. Though Ratzinger does not advert to it, conscience here would seem to be closely related to the virtue of prudence.[17] The two levels are distinct but interrelated. One must act according to one's judgment or conviction, even if it is objectively wrong—but one may be guilty for making the wrong decision. The guilt lies somewhere else, not for judging something right that is in fact objectively wrong, but deeper, "in the desolation of my being that makes me insensible to the voice of truth and its appeal to my inner self".[18] For this reason, criminals like Hitler and Stalin are guilty and cannot be excused for following their "erroneous consciences".

There is a final dimension that Ratzinger mentions in an epilogue, that of grace, the forgiveness of God once we recognize our guilt. It is the divine power of expiation, which, as the Greeks had already recognized, was needed to wash away our guilt. Without attention to this, the real core of the Christian message, truth can become a yoke on our shoulders too heavy for us to bear.

3. Conscience and the objective moral law

Like so much of Ratzinger's writing, this essay could be described as seminal. Though unfinished, it contains seeds that need time and the rich humus of other theological minds in order to ripen and flourish. It is the result of a lifetime of reflection on and existential wrestling with the question. In my view, it is a major contribution to moral

---

[17] See Pieper, *Traktat über die Klugheit*, especially pp. 23–44.
[18] *WWM* 58.

theology, a subject that we have hardly touched on in the above but one where Ratzinger has already made significant contributions, albeit also of a similar seminal nature. These latter need to be read in conjunction with this essay, in particular his reflections on the existence of an objective morality that before the modern period mankind universally recognized, namely, "the conviction that man's Being contains an imperative; the conviction that he does not himself *invent* morality on the basis of calculations of expediency but rather *finds* it already present in the essence of things."[19] This conviction is common to all man's great religious and wisdom traditions, which flow like tributaries into the great Christian vision of reality. "The ethical vision of the Christian faith is not in fact something specific to Christianity but is the synthesis of the great ethical intuitions of mankind from a new center that holds them all together."[20] There is also much that needs to be developed and further refined, not least the second level of conscience, which is too brief to be satisfactory.[21] Whatever its limitations, the recovery of what Ratzinger calls the ontological level of conscience has profound implications for moral theology, for politics, and, especially, for the possibility and right of the Church to engage in mission.[22]

---

[19] *TPE* 28–29; there Ratzinger takes up and develops the insights of C. S. Lewis, *The Abolition of Man* (London: Oxford University Press, 1943).

[20] *TPE* 37; *PCM* 43–66. In stressing what is common to the sapiential traditions of mankind, Ratzinger may have let himself open to the criticism that he does not give sufficient attention to what is specifically Christian— that newness which is our life in Christ; cf. Servais Pinckaers, O.P., *The Sources of Christian Ethics*, trans. from the 3rd ed. by Sr. Mary Thomas Noble, O.P. (Washington, D.C.: Catholic University of America Press, 1995).

[21] See my criticism of this particular weakness in his account of conscience in appendix 1.

[22] *WWM* 53–54; also pp. 30–33.

In a homily on Deuteronomy 4:7 ("What great nation is there that has a god so near to it as the LORD our God is to us, whenever we call upon him?"), Ratzinger links conscience with the Eucharist. The link is by means of a reflection on the nature of the revealed Law of God, the moral law. The Old Testament text rejoices that God is close to his people in a unique way through the Law he gave to Israel through Moses. Through the Law, he speaks to them and they respond to him. His Law enables them to build up a social and political order that breaks new ground, indicating how man should live. Through the Law, God has, as it were, "drawn back the veil from the riddles of human life and replied to the obscure questionings of men of all ages: Where do we come from? Where are we going? What must we do?" [23] Ratzinger notes how astounded we are by this joy in the Law, since we are used to seeing law as an imposition, a burden that oppresses man. But for Israel, the Law set them free for the truth, free from the burden of uncertainty. "For man, the will of God is not a foreign force of external origin, but the actual orientation of his own being. Thus the revelation of God's will is the revelation of what our own being truly wishes—it is a gift." [24] The Law became a burden "the moment it was no longer lived out from within but was broken down into a series of obligations external in their origins and their nature." [25] The Lord, however, has told us in no uncertain terms that the Law is within us. "It speaks to us in our conscience."

---

[23] J. Ratzinger, *God Is Near Us: The Eucharist, the Heart of Life*, ed. Stephan Otto Horn and Vinzenz Pfnur, trans. Henry Taylor (San Francisco: Ignatius Press, 2003), p. 104. I am grateful to Joseph Murphy for reminding me of this text.

[24] Ibid.

[25] Ibid., p. 105.

Echoing Deuteronomy 30:14, we can say that "conscience is the inner aspect of the Lord's presence, which alone can render us capable of receiving the eucharistic presence.... Faith in Christ simply renders the inmost part of our being, our conscience, once more articulate." [26]

4. Conscience and other religions

Ratzinger's theology of the non-Christians religions [27] is, needless to mention, richer than the public discussion on *Dominus Iesus* might lead the unwary to suspect. The starting point of this theology is his understanding of human beings as essentially cultural beings. He understands culture, not as something fixed, but as something dynamic and constantly open to change. Because people today think of culture as something static, acquired by the accident of birth in a particular community, most attempts at a theology of religions assume that the world religions, which form the core of the great cultural traditions of mankind, are likewise to be conceived as static entities. Thus it is recommended that each one make the best of whatever religion he happens to born into, in the hope that all paths lead to the one God.

Is this shortchanging man?

Culture [28] is the historically formed, spiritual/linguistic, moral/symbolic environment (or womb) needed for the development of each human being's potential. Equally true,

[26] Ibid.

[27] See in particular *TT* and his book *Many Religions—One Covenant: Israel, the Church, and the World*, trans. Graham Harrison, with a foreword by Scott Hahn (San Francisco: Ignatius Press, 1999).

[28] See Ratzinger's definition above in Chapter Three, note 5. See also his *Unterwegs zu Jesus Christus* (Augsburg: Sankt Ulrich Verlag, 2005), pp. 41–43 for a more complete discussion of the nature of culture.

though largely ignored, is the fact that each one of us also has the potential for transcending his own particular culture thanks to his capacity for God. While culture is always particular, yet at the same time each culture is open to the universal. Thus the great literatures of the world are at the same time intensely particular and yet universal in scope. (Shakespeare, for example, is uniquely English, indeed Elizabethan, and yet he is universal in appeal because he plumbs the depths of the human soul.) At the core of each ancient culture is a shared cult, religion, worship, which, rooted in some primordial experience of the ground of all being, defines the inner character of that culture. But cultures also exist in history and so are subject to change (both in the sense of enrichment or of decay) depending on whether they are open or closed to the universality of truth. Further, cultures interact.

> Each particular culture not only lives out its own experience of God, the world, and man, but on its path it necessarily encounters other cultural agencies and has to react to their quite different experiences. This results, depending always on the degree to which the cultural agent may be closed or open, inwardly narrow or broad in outlook, in that culture's own perceptions and values being deepened and purified. . . . A process of this kind can in fact lead to a breaking open of the silent alienation of man from the truth and from himself that exists within that culture.[29]

"Can or must a man simply make the best of the religion that happens to fall to his share, in the form in which it is actually practiced around him?" Ratzinger asks. "Or must he not, whatever happens, be one who seeks, who strives to purify his conscience and, thus, move toward—at the

---

[29] TT 63.

very least—the purer forms of his own religion?"[30] It is conscience, in its primal or ontological sense, that seeks to purify itself, that seeks to go beyond inherited practice and values, that enables one to transcend one's culture and its religious and moral values. To the extent that cultures have this "Advent quality", that is, to the extent that they are seeking to know the truth beyond them as the Jews were looking for the Hope of Israel, to that extent they are dynamic and ultimately open to the self-revelation of God in Christ through the Church. But, Ratzinger adds, the same dynamic quality is also to be found in a certain sense within Christianity itself. Christianity "is not simply a network of institutions and ideas we have to hand on but a seeking ever in faith for faith's inmost dept, for the real encounter with Christ." And he adds:

> In that way—to say it again—in Judaism the "poor of Israel" developed; in that way they would have to develop, again and again, within the Church; and in that way they can and they should develop in other religions: it is the dynamic of the conscience and of the silent presence of God in it that is leading religions toward one another and guiding people onto the path to God, not the canonizing of what already exists, so that people are excused from any deeper searching.[31]

5. Conclusion

In the wake of *Humanae Vitae*, an understanding of conscience emerged within theology and was adopted by a

---

[30] *TT* 54.

[31] Ibid. Regarding the "Advent quality" of Christianity, see the first 1964 sermon reproduced in his book *Vom Sinn des Christseins* (Munich: Kösel-Verlag, 2005).

number of episcopal conferences that in effect justified an opposition between the teaching authority of the Church and the individual believer. Such a notion of conscience could fulfill that function only because it was inherently ambiguous and resonated strongly with contemporary cultural trends. It combined the strand of an impoverished tradition of Catholic moral theology that affirmed the obligation to follow one's conscience, even if erroneous, with the subjectivity of modernity. Since one cannot in practice ignore the principle of contradiction, which is what the compromise involved, many chose to do what they wanted to do and in effect rejected the authority of the Church.

The debate in moral theology that resulted from the rejection of *Humanae Vitae* was not about sexual morality in the first instance but about the nature of morality itself.[32] This was due to the denial of objective morality by the breaching of moral absolutes, namely, the denial of the teaching that there are certain human acts that of their nature are intrinsically wrong,[33] the most ancient of moral insights that human wisdom has always upheld. The practical and theoretical denial of this teaching means in effect that there is no real limit to what man, legislator or scientist, citizen or believer, may do, no way to offset the threat of totalitarianism or the control of the many by the few experts, except by way of personal conscience, in the full sense of the term, as represented by such people as the Lucayan girl (in Schneider's

[32] For a perceptive account and analysis of that debate, see Janet E. Smith, *Humanae Vitae: A Generation Later* (Washington, D.C.: Catholic University of America Press, 1991), in particular chaps. 6 and 7, pp. 161–229.

[33] Cf. *Humanae Vitae* 14; see also *Veritatis Splendor* 79–93, the most recent authoritative teaching on that debate.

novel), Bartholomé de Las Casas, Sir Thomas More, Andrey Sakharov.[34]

But there is an important message of hope in the newly recovered understanding of conscience and morality outlined by Ratzinger. Because man as creature, made in the image and likeness of God, is by definition, as it were, capable of truth,[35] the public distortion of truth can never totally succeed irrespective of the naked power that distortion momentarily wields. It can be overcome by the powerlessness of conscience that suffers for the truth, in other words, by the mystery of the Cross. For this reason, the Church as the place where faith awakens conscience is the only abiding bulwark against the corruption of society and the totalitarian tendencies inherent in all secular authority, not least in modern democracies dominated by moral relativism. The Church's task, to repeat again what was quoted earlier, is "to break open the prism of positivism and awaken man's receptivity to the truth, to God, and thus to the power of conscience".[36] For this reason Sakharov once said: "The closure of half of all the churches would deal no lesser blow to the country than the closure of all scientific institutes would do."[37]

---

[34] See Ratzinger's appreciation of Sakharov, whose empty chair he was invited to fill, in an address given on the occasion of his becoming a *membre associé étranger* at the *Académie des Sciences Morales et Politiques* of the *Institut de France* on the November 7, 1992, in Paris (reprinted in *WWM* 13–24).

[35] In his address to the participants at the International Conference on the Human Genome, November 19, 2005, Pope Benedict XVI recalled the same truth: "God's image is deeply impressed in the soul of the human being, the voice of whose conscience it is far from easy to silence" (Zenit).

[36] *TPE* 55.

[37] As quoted in H. Staudinger and W. Behler, eds., *Chance und Risiko der Gegenwart: Eine kritische Analyse der wissenschaftlich-technischen Welt* (Paderborn: Schöningh, 1976), p. 340.

Appendix 1

A CRITIQUE

Ratzinger may have left himself open to some misunderstanding by not giving sufficient attention to the role of the virtue of prudence and by not examining in greater depth what he called "the second level of conscience". Further, granted that Ratzinger was anxious to show the interrelatedness between the Church's teaching authority and our *primordial conscience*, the relationship still remains to be teased out in greater detail, as does the role of other, more humble moral authorities in education and in the training for virtue. On the other hand, Peter Fonk[1] admits the value of Ratzinger's stress on *anamnesis* but presents what he calls a more acceptable Aristotelian alternative, namely, the art of the helmsman. This, he claims, is the ability to apply general rules and principles in uncharted waters. Fonk takes up Rahner's attempt ("Plädoyer für eine namenlose Tugend") to apply this Aristotelian starting point to the present. Rahner sees the path to truth in the mean between

[1] See Peter Fonk, "Die Kunst des Steuermanns: Aristoteles' Beitrag zu einer theologischen Lehre vom Gewissen", in K. Arntz and P. Schallenberg, eds., *Ethik zwischen Anspruch und Zuspruch* (Fribourg: Universitätsverlag; Freiburg im Breisgau: Herder, 1996), pp. 284–300.

the two extremes "of tired relativism and stubborn fanaticism".[2] Fonk suggests that this existentially significant virtue be entitled the "moral power of judgment" (*moralische Urteilskraft*). What Fonk seems to have done, it seems to me, is to describe the virtue of *prudence* insofar as it relates to the second level of conscience, that of judgment, which is always directed to particular situations and which presupposes that life itself is literally a stretch of unexplored waters (see references to the works of Josef Pieper above).[3] It seems that Fonk has failed to distinguish the first, or ontological, level of conscience from the second level, that of judgment—and their interrelatedness—which failure Ratzinger rightly says is the cause of many unacceptable theses regarding conscience.[4] This is all the more strange, since Fonk chides Plato (and by implication Ratzinger) for failing to make the distinction between speculative and practical reason, when it seems to me that Fonk, following Rahner, confuses the two. The uncharted waters into which the helmsman steers is not the area of *articulating ethical rules and moral principles* (the work of the legislator and of the philosopher or theologian). It is the drama of everyday life, above all when the unexpected happens, where each of us has to learn how to apply these principles, most of which are general and flexible guides (mostly of a positive nature) and some of which are universal and so admitting of no exception (and are mostly of a negative nature), principles that arise from

---

[2] Fonk, "Kunst des Steuermanns", pp. 299–300.

[3] See chap. 5, n. 3 above. On the classical expression of the relationship between the primordial conscience (*anamnesis* or *synderesis*) and conscience (*conscientia*) in the narrow sense as exercised in the virtue of prudence, see Saint Thomas Aquinas, *STh* II–II, 47, art. 6 (in particular ad 3) and art. 15. Thomas discusses the nature of *synderesis* in *STh* I, 79, arts. 12 and 13.

[4] Cf. *WWM* 4.

our common humanity and that once articulated, are recognized by the ontological level of conscience. The Church's teaching authority is directed to these principles and laws, which are not invented but discovered by reason and confirmed (clarified) by revelation. She does seem to play the role of midwife.

Chapter Six

THE GERMAN POPE:
GUILT BY ASSOCIATION

*We are all well aware of the evil that emerged from our Home-
land during the twentieth century, and we acknowledge it with
shame and suffering. During these days [World Youth Day,
Cologne], thanks be to God, it has become quite evident that
there was and is another Germany, a Land of singular human,
cultural and spiritual resources. I hope and pray that these
resources, thanks, not least, to the events of recent days, may
once more spread throughout the world!*

— *Pope Benedict XVI, Farewell Address*
World Youth Day 2005

Edith Stein, writing to Pius XI the year Hitler rose to power
(1933), appealed to the Pope to speak out publicly against
the persecution of the Jews in Germany. In her letter, she
also warned: "The war against Catholicism develops stealth-
ily and with less brutal systems than against Judaism, but
it is also systematic." [1] This "war against Catholicism" was

---

[1] The letter, first made public in 2003, is the subject of the book edited
by Philippe Chenaux and Angela Ales Bello entitled *Edith Stein e il Nazismo*
(Rome: Città Nuova, 2005). On the fate of that letter when it arrived in
Rome, see Pinchas E. Lapide, *Rom und die Juden: Pius XII. und die Judenverfolgung*, 3rd ed. (Bad Schussenried: Gerhard Hess Verlag, 2005), p. 56.

documented in detail in a 565-page book entitled *The Persecution of the Catholic Church in the Third Reich*, by an anonymous author and published by Burns, Oates (London) in 1940.[2] This is an aspect of modern German history that is usually ignored in the Anglo-Saxon world, as is the fact that many Catholic priests were incarcerated in the concentration camps—some 2800 alone in Dachau[3]—while 354 names have been recorded to date of those who died directly as a result of Hitler's reign of terror.[4] Ratzinger himself, in an interview in 1993, recalled various attacks on priests and nuns that he knew about in his youth, such as the bomb thrown into the residence of the Augustinian Canons Regular in Traunstein before the Ratzinger family had moved to the town.[5] Taking about his attitude as a schoolboy seminarian, he said: "We certainly wanted the defeat of Nazism, there was no doubt about that. One thing was clear: the Nazis wanted, after the war, to eliminate the Church.

[2] It was reprinted several times and published in paperback in 2003. I am grateful to Msgr. James O'Brien for drawing my attention to this invaluable work. Included in the documentation is a pastoral letter issued by the German bishops at Fulda on August 19, 1938, where they state inter alia: "They [the Nazis] are trying to restrict us on every side, to bleed our Catholic life to death. Yea, more: they aim at the complete overthrow of the Catholic Church on German soil, and even the entire elimination of Christianity of whatever sort, and the introduction in its place of a form of belief which is utterly alien to the true faith in God and belief in a future life" (p. 31). The book also reproduces a number of anti-Catholic caricatures, including two attacking Cardinal Pacelli, later Pope Pius XII.

[3] Cf., for example, Johann Maria Lenz, *Christus in Dachau oder Christus der Siege: Ein religiöses Volksbuch und ein kirchengeschichtliches Zeugnis* (Vienna, 1957); English translation, *Christ in Dachau; or, Christ Victorious* (Vienna, 1960). The last surviving priest who had been incarcerated in Dachau said that he never felt closer to God than in Dachau (see *The Word*, October 2005).

[4] Cf. Helmut Moll, *Die katholischen deutschen Märtyrer des 20. Jahrhunderts: Ein Verzeichnis*, 4th rev. ed. (Paderborn: Schöningh, 2005).

[5] Cf. *Inside the Vatican*, May 2005, p. 39.

There would definitely be no more priests. This was one reason we [seminarians] longed for their defeat."[6] This does not fit into the rather black-and-white picture of the Second World War that owes much to the comic-book depictions of the heroic British outwitting the evil German soldiers that were the staple diet of youngsters like myself for at least two decades after the war.[7] The result was the suspicion that perhaps all Germans were at least crypto-Nazis; that all were in some sense responsible for the atrocities committed by Hitler. All were guilty by association.

This applied above all to the Bavarians, since Hitler rose to prominence in Munich and, after he seized power, held his monster rallies in Nuremberg, in the predominantly Lutheran part of Franconia, which was incorporated into the Bavarian Free State. And it was in the Bavarian Alps near Bechtesgarten that the Führer spent his holidays. It should not be forgotten that Hitler used nationalism and patriotism—powerful sentiments good in themselves but capable of turning demonic[8]—to his own evil ends. As a result, Germans themselves sometimes felt not a little ambiguous about what is in fact innocent folklore, while for the Anglo-Saxons that folklore simply evoked the Nazi past.

---

[6] Ibid., pp. 40–41. See Volker Laube, *Das Erzbischöfliche Studienseminar St. Michael in Traunstein und sein Archiv* (Regensburg: Schnell und Steiner Verlag, 2006), which, on the basis of the available documentation, demonstrates the palpable anti-Nazi ethos of Ratzinger's boarding school (or minor seminary), as recognized by the Nazis themselves.

[7] I am forever grateful to my music teacher at secondary school (Christian Brothers' College, Cork), the late Michael O'Callaghan, who, in introducing us raw youths to the world of Bach and Beethoven, Schubert and Mozart, also unintentionally molded my own image of things German, thus counteracting the image of the comic books.

[8] Cf. C. S. Lewis, *The Four Loves* (London: G. Bles, 1960), in particular the first chapter, on the subhuman loves.

Bavaria is not only largely traditional, but it is predominantly Catholic. Indeed, Hitler was born in Braunau, over the border in Austria, only a few miles away from Marktl-am-Inn, where Ratzinger was born. And Hitler, too, was baptized a Catholic.

At the time of Hitler's *Putsch*, Munich in fact was a secular city with a history of radicalism in art, literature, and politics—mostly at enmity with traditional Catholicism—while Nuremberg was predominantly Protestant and, so, anti-Catholic. And yet, Bavarian Catholicism is particularly susceptible to guilt by association—even though the Archbishop of Munich, Michael Cardinal Faulhaber, was one of the German bishops most outspoken in his opposition to Hitler and his policies,[9] while the Catholic men of Munich were to a great extent under the sway of the charismatic Father Rupert Mayer, S.J. (beatified by John Paul II), chaplain to the Jesuit Men's Sodality of Our Lady in Munich. Fearful of his influence, the Nazis forbade Father Mayer to preach. He refused, was arrested, imprisoned, and eventually placed under house arrest (in Ettal

[9] Recent research, I have been informed, indicates that initially Faulhaber sought a *modus vivendi* with Hitler and did not in fact speak openly against anti-Semitism. His most outspoken attack, it is claimed, was against euthanasia and its associated policy of eugenics. This does not tally with that which Alfred Rosenberg noted in his diary: "The evil Cardinal Faulhaber spoke in Munich and attacked my writings" (H.-G. Seraphim, *Das politische Tagebuch Alfred Rosenbergs aus den Jahren 1934/1935 und 1939/1940* [Göttingen: Musterschmidt, 1956], p. 56, as quoted in Joachim C. Fest, *Das Gesicht des Dritten Reiches* [Munich: Piper, 1963], p. 235). Karl Stern confirms this in his testimony to the powerful impact Cardinal Faulhaber's Advent sermons, December 1933, entitled "Jewry and Christianity", made on him as a Jew. "All he did was clarify the birth certificate of Jesus of Nazareth, who was a Jew in the flesh, and to reassert the oneness, the complete organic unity of the God of the Church and the God of the Patriarchs and Kings of Israel" (Karl Stern, *The Pillar of Fire: A Personal Story of a Spiritual Voyage from Judaism to Catholicism* [London: Michael Joseph, 1951], p. 160; Image Books edition, 1959, p. 157).

Abbey).[10] (They would have liquidated him, but they feared an uprising if they tried.) The fact is that those parts of Germany, such as Bavaria and South Oldenburg, that had retained a strong traditional Catholic piety were the areas where Nazism was weakest and resistance to it was strongest.[11] This was reflected in the voting pattern for the 1932 elections: "Wherever there were most Catholics there were least votes for the Nazi Party; wherever there were least Catholics there were most votes for the Nazi Party".[12] In addition, Adenauer recalled that: "National Socialism found the strongest mental and moral opposition in those parts of Germany which, whether Catholic or Protestant, had been least affected by socialism and the doctrine of Karl Marx."[13]

[10] Walter Rupp, S.J., *Rupert Mayer SJ: Der Apostel Münchens* (Munich: Pressereferat d. Erzdiözese München und Freising, 1986). Describing the Catholics whose exemplary lives influenced his conversion from Lutheranism, Heinrich Schlier, the great exegete, describes the impression the incarcerated Father Rupert Mayer, S.J., left on him: "He was like an imprisoned lion, who impatiently lashed at the bars of his cage. How he awaited the day when he would be free to exercise his ministry" ("Kurze Rechenschaft", in Karl Hardt, ed., *Bekenntnis zur katholischen Kirche*, 2nd ed. [Würzburg: Echter-Verlag, 1955], p. 171); see also Cardinal Faulhaber's powerful sermon to the men's sodality on the arrest of Father Mayer in *The Persecution of the Church* (see n. 2 above), appendix 3.

[11] For a description of the "Latin cosmopolitanism" that makes Bavaria so different from the rest of Germany and of the harmony that prevailed between Jews and their Catholic neighbors in Bavaria before the rise of anti-Semitism after the First World War, see Stern, *Pillar of Fire*, passim, but in particular chap. 12, pp. 126–32, and chap. 19, pp. 179–87.

[12] *Saint Austin Review*, September–October 2005, p. 17, commenting on two maps of Germany that reveal at a glance the fact that support for Hitler was lowest among Catholics. One showed the distribution of the Catholic population in Germany according to the 1934 census; the other showed the percentage of National Socialist votes in the 1932 election.

[13] Konrad Adenauer, *Memoirs 1945–53*, trans. Beate Ruhm von Oppen (London: Widenfeld and Nicolson, 1966), p. 40.

When the Bavarian Joseph Ratzinger was elected to the See of Peter as Pope Benedict XVI, it was no surprise to find the English tabloids appealing to the worst prejudices of their readers: "From Nazi to Papa Ratzi" was one headline; another was "From Hitler Youth to . . . Papa Ratzi". Even some of the American, British, and Irish quality papers (not to mention the radio talk shows) fed into it.[14] Their justification, it seems, was a report by John Allen, whose biography of Ratzinger we will examine below (epilogue), claiming to have found evidence that the present pope had indeed been a member of the Hitler Youth. This item of news was initially presented as though the young Ratzinger had actually *enrolled* in the Hitler Youth, when in fact every single German youth of a certain age was without exception automatically registered as a member.[15] They had no choice. Ratzinger did not attend any Hitler Youth meetings. This misinformation was corrected almost within a few days. But the damage was done.

Allen should have known that the previous year Pope John Paul II had chosen Joseph Cardinal Ratzinger to be his representative as papal legate at the celebrations to mark the sixtieth anniversary of D-Day on the beaches of Normandy, a highly symbolic action by the Polish pope, who himself hailed from a country crushed mercilessly by the Nazis during the war. On that historic day in Normandy,

[14] This initial reaction soon gave way to a more positive assessment. Nicholas Boyle, professor of German literature and intellectual history, University of Cambridge, more astutely commented: "One advantage of our having a German Pope is that the British may at last begin to get a better understanding of Germany" (*The Tablet*, May 7, 2005, p. 4).

[15] In a television interview for an RTÉ documentary on Pope Benedict XVI, Ratzinger's brother, Georg, clarified that there were two groups of Hitler Youth, those who joined voluntarily and those, like himself and Joseph, who were compelled to join.

Cardinal Ratzinger in his speech on war and peace captured the gratitude of many Germans at the time who saw the landing of the Allies as a sign of hope. He also depicted the precise nature of the diabolically political ambiguity in which innocent Germans were forced to live at the time. It was a State ruled by a criminal, who turned the State's legal system based on justice and the need for public order into a means of committing gross injustices and crimes against humanity.[16]

The hand of Providence is easily discernable in Ratzinger's life. The day after his Inauguration Mass, Pope Benedict held a special audience for German pilgrims. That day happened to be the sixtieth anniversary of the ending of the war in Italy. Six decades after the German army was routed, a German pope addressed a horde of German pilgrims armed only with faith and loyalty and love. One of the reasons he chose the name was to honor Benedict XV, whose warning to the Allies after the First World War was tragically ignored.[17] Benedict XV had foreseen that the postwar settlement involved nothing less than the humiliation of Germany, for which the rest of Europe would one day pay a heavy price.[18] That price was the rise of Hitler, whose initial popularity rested on his attempts to restore German self-esteem as well as the German economy, the former being the more significant of the two. A people or nation cannot live without self-esteem.

[16] See the text of his speech on June 6, 2004, in Joseph Ratzinger, *Values in a Time of Upheaval*, trans. Brian McNeil, C.R.V. (San Francisco: Ignatius Press, 2006), pp. 117–22.

[17] See the *Message of His Holiness Pope Benedict XVI for the Celebration of the World Day of Peace*, January 1, 2006, no. 2.

[18] It is interesting to note that, in an impromptu aside to his talk on Psalm 122 (123) during his Wednesday audience on June 15, 2005, the present pope called for the mobilization and prayers of believers for harassed and humiliated individuals *and nations*.

Nationalism and patriotism are sentiments that express it. However, as Benedict XVI points out, they are relative values, which, when absolutized, become diabolical.[19]

The election of Pope Benedict XVI may yet give Germany that self-esteem which Hitler parodied.[20] The gradual realization that the accusations about the Pope's supposedly "Nazi Youth" were without any foundation might serve to draw attention to an even more important fact, namely, that not all Germans can be tarred with the same brush. Count less anonymous Germans were innocent of any taint of Nazism. They suffered in varying degrees under the Nazi terror. They were acutely conscious, as Edith Stein was in 1933, that Nazism was essentially anti-Christian and, in particular, anti-Catholic. Among them were the Ratzinger family.[21] The

[19] In his address at the vigil of World Youth Day, August 20, 2005, Pope Benedict XVI pointed out in one of his potent statements that "Making absolute what is not absolute but relative [such as race or nation] is called totalitarianism." See also Lewis, *Four Loves*, chap. I, on the subhuman love of patriotism and its demonic potential.

[20] This is said, notwithstanding the fact that, as has been observed, "the official reaction of the German Catholic Church to the spectacular election of a German pope was, to put it mildly, restrained" (Martin Mosebach, *International Herald Tribune*, May 3, 2005). Mosebach's analysis of why the reaction of a predominantly middle-class Church was downbeat at best is most perceptive. The German Church, he claims, is ever afraid of "losing their voice in the democratic consensus", while most German Catholic clergy are intimidated by contemporary culture. Mosebach also points out that Benedict is strikingly un-German in many respects (and certainly does not fit the Bavarian stereotype beloved of non-Bavarians), though "his German is beautiful". In the meantime, the Pope made his first visit to his homeland for the World Youth Day in Cologne, when he won the hearts and minds of many skeptical Germans, though without making any definitive breakthrough, it would seem. His historic visit to Bavaria in September 2006 left a more lasting impression.

[21] For the most comprehensive account of his youth and his experiences during the war, see the interview Cardinal Ratzinger gave to Robert Moynihan in 1993 (first published in *Inside the Vatican* in 2001 and reprinted in the same periodical in May 2005, pp. 34–41).

Pope's father was a policeman charged with the task of keeping order in the local communities. He represented the State. He was responsible for justice being done in his small area.[22] So upright and conscientious was he that at least on one occasion an attempt was made on his life. According to an oral tradition among his students, Ratzinger's father had intervened to protect a family who were being ostracized by the local community, thereby earning the wrath of the tight-knit community, one of whom decided to take revenge on him. But when the would-be assassin came to the family's house that evening and looked in through the window, he saw the family kneeling in prayer. He admitted that he could not bring himself to shoot a father at prayer with his wife and children.

In an interview in 1993 given to Robert Moynihan,[23] Ratzinger pointed out that his father, a man of superior intellect and strong convictions, with an interest in modern history and politics, did not approve of the incorporation of Bavaria into Bismarck's greater Germany and so a fortiori opposed the Nazis and did so publicly. A month before Hitler came to power, his father moved the family from the larger town of Tittmoning to the more rural Aschau, knowing that they would be safer there. Even there, however, the father came under pressure from the Nazis to make life difficult for the clergy and nuns. He resisted this pressure to such an extent that the Nazis bypassed him and sub-

---

[22] Ratzinger's father's uncle, Georg Ratzinger, was a priest and elected public representative. He championed the rights of the peasants and simple people in general and was evidently held in high esteem in the family and by his grand nephew in particular (see *SE* 45). The concern of his grand-uncle Georg Ratzinger for justice and the poor evidently influenced not only Ratzinger's father but the future cardinal and pope as well.

[23] See n. 21 above.

sequently gave orders of this nature to his second-in-command. When the father nonetheless got to know of these attacks, he warned the parish priest.

It is not difficult to imagine the moral dilemma facing Ratzinger's father as Nazism began to cast its dark shadow over the small world for which he was responsible and as the State he represented became a robber's den. He and his family were convinced anti-Nazis. In his final year as a policeman, he took more and more sick leave, spending much of his time with his family, in particular with Joseph, until he could finally retire. Joseph Ratzinger's depiction of the diabolical legal ambiguity of Nazi Germany was something he had himself experienced firsthand—including the "disappearance" of five disabled neighbors, one of whom was a cousin with Down's Syndrome.[24] He also admits that, though many Christians heroically resisted the terror, many others failed to show sufficient resistance. "There were of course a good number of Christians, some of whose names we know and some who have remained nameless, who opposed the demonic forces with the power of their Christian conscience. But on the whole the power of temptation was stronger; those who just went along with things left a clear path for evil." [25]

Ratzinger's short autobiography—more accurately, a collection of memoirs—was, like most of his writings, probably jotted down over a very short space of time, during whatever free hours he could spare after his official tasks as cardinal prefect had been completed. It is written in essay style, short and rather sweeping at times, with just sufficient details

---

[24] Cf. Cardinal Joseph Ratzinger, "The Likeness of God in the Human Being", in *Dolentium Hominum*, no. 34 (1997): 17.

[25] See *TT* 140.

for a charcoal sketch to emerge rather than a full portrait in oils. Living in the shadow of Salzburg—and of Mozart—he grew up in soil that was European rather than simply German. He notes the various influences on his homeland that molded his youth, such as the ancient Celts and Romans, pagan and Christian, as well as the missionaries from Ireland, England, and Gaul.

The young Ratzinger was fortunate to have benefited from the remnants of an educational system based on the ancient classics (Greek and Latin)—the foundation of the great German intellectual tradition—which the Nazis began to dismantle as soon as they came to power. At secondary school, his mind and heart were opened to the great thinkers of Western civilization, thus laying the foundations for his later theology and his intellectual independence. Noting the fact that not one of his teachers of Greek and Latin had joined the Nazi Party, despite considerable pressure to do so, he commented: "In retrospect it seems to me that an education in Greek and Latin antiquity created a mental attitude that resisted seduction by a totalitarian ideology." [26]

In a word, the influence of the Nazi terror on the young Ratzinger (and presumably his fellow students) was negative. He recoiled from its dark shadow. Asked in a fairly recent interview about how the Nazi period had influenced him, Ratzinger replied: "In two ways, I would say. First, we were made more aware of our faith. . . . And then second, I would say that we saw a certain anti-Christian vision of the world that, in the final analysis, showed itself to be anti-human and absurd, [though], at first, being in power, it displayed itself as the great hope of humanity. And as a result, I learned to have a certain reserve with regard to

[26] *MM* 23.

the reigning ideologies."[27] However, as the war effort was about to collapse, and even schoolboys were enlisted to help the military effort, he too was sucked to the edge of the vortex that had liquidated millions of innocents and caused devastation from the Atlantic to the Urals. Although he had not participated in any serious military action, he was incarcerated in a prisoner-of-war camp for a short while by the Americans. He, too, knew from an early age what it was to be innocent and yet considered guilty. When the war was over and he could return to his theological studies—the priest in charge of his formation in the seminary had spent a number of years in the Dachau concentration camp—he did so in a country that had been brought to its knees and in a Church that on the whole had resisted[28] and finally overcome the Nazi terror. It was a good time to be

[27] Interview with Robert Moynihan, *Inside the Vatican*, May 2005, p. 41.

[28] After the collapse of the Nazi regime, according to one historian, there was general recognition of the moral resistance of the Catholic Church: see Hubert Gruber, *Nationalsozialistisches Regime und katholische Kirche: Ein Bericht in Quellen* (Paderborn: Schöningh, 2004). Helmuth James Count von Moltke was one of the leaders of the German resistance and founder of the Kreisauer Circle (which included Father Alfred Delp, S.J.), a conspiracy to assassinate Hitler. Their attempted coup on July 20, 1944, failed, and all were brutally executed in Plötzensee, Berlin. Von Moltke's letter, reproduced in the *Frankfurter Allgemeine Zeitung* on July 20, 1974, was addressed to one of his English relatives and written while on a diplomatic mission in neutral Sweden. In it he attempted to counteract his English relatives' reproach that there was no organized resistance to the Nazi tyranny comparable to that in France or Italy. After explaining why organized resistance was so very difficult in Germany, he went on to say that there was, despite the Nazi system of terror and spies, considerable resistance, and in the first place that of the Catholic Church. In this context, the essay by Kenneth L. Woodward in defense of Pius XII in *Newsweek*, March 30, 1998, is also of interest. See also Pinchas E. Lapide, *Rom und die Juden: Papst Pius XII und die Judenverfolgung*, 3rd ed. (Bad Schussenried: Gerhard Hess Verlag, 2005), which corroborates, on the basis of documentary evidence, the testimony of von Molke to the widespread Catholic resistance, which Pope Pius XII encouraged to the best of his ability.

a Catholic in Germany. "Not only was Catholicism numer-
ically dominant in the Federal Republic—while the over-
whelming Protestantism of East Germany was of little
consequence beside Communism and established atheism—
but the moral and intellectual authority of the Catholic
Church was also enhanced, both by its ability to appeal to
a record of resistance, even if not particularly effective resistance, to the Nazi regime, and by the bankruptcy of the
central tradition of national bureaucracy." [29]

Ratzinger was one of millions of innocent Germans who,
though they had rejected Nazism, yet suffered in various
degrees from its evil effects. These included the many young
men who, like himself and his elder brother, Georg, were
conscripted to serve in the army, some of whom did so for
genuinely patriotic reasons. All of them suffered from the
horrors of war. After the defeat of Nazism, all Germans
then had to live with the memory of what had been done
in the name of Germany by their fellow compatriots. They
experienced guilt by association. Perhaps the mentality of
such good, ordinary, down-to-earth people was summed
up by Konrad Adenauer, the first German chancellor of
the newly created German Federal Republic.

> During the National Socialist period I was often ashamed
> to be a German, ashamed to the depths of my soul.... I
> had learned of the atrocities committed by Germans against
> Germans, and of the crimes perpetrated against mankind.
> Yet after the catastrophe, when I saw how the German peo-
> ple bore their terrible fate, endured in hunger, cold, need

[29] Nicholas Boyle, "The New Spirit of Germany", *The Tablet*, May 7,
2005, p. 4. This is a most perceptive account of the Germany—Western
Germany—that formed the background for Ratzinger's intellectual development and of the influence that environment had on his thinking, particularly
on his political thought.

and death an existence temporarily without hope for the future, in complete political incompetence, despised by all the peoples of the earth; when I saw the German people suffering this fate in patient strength that seemed stronger than their misery, then I was proud once more to be a German. I was proud of the fortitude with which the German people bore their fate, proud to see each one suffering without despair, struggling not to go under but to save himself and his family from this present distress for the sake of a better future.[30]

This was the kind of Germany that formed the present pope and which he in turn helped to form. In doing so, he also helped to transform the Church universal. He was one of a whole generation of great German thinkers who left their mark not only on theological scholarship but on the whole Church through the influence they played at the Second Vatican Council. They were conscious of the fact that Catholics in general did not support the Nazi terror and that many had suffered, including countless priests, as already mentioned. Nonetheless, the guilt by association lasted. But this in turn produced what must be one of the most distinctive aspects of Ratzinger's character, his humble courage—that fortitude which Adenauer recognized in his people after the war. It is his courage as a writer and public figure that makes Joseph Ratzinger the conscience of our age.

When, as mentioned already, he was elected to the French Academy to replace the Soviet dissident Andrey Sakharov, the French Immortals were in fact paying tribute to the greatest living "dissident" in Western Europe: Joseph Cardinal Ratzinger. It is true that, in the first place, his election to the Academy was a public recognition of the unique

<hr>

[30] Adenauer, *Memoirs*, p. 38 (translation slightly altered).

scholarly contribution he had made—and continues to make—to political thought through his writings on contemporary moral and political developments. His is an independent and original contribution that is rooted in a profound theological vision, Catholic in the most all-embracing sense of the term. But, above all, his election to the Academy was their way of giving public recognition to one of the few voices of sanity in a world that denies the very possibility of truth, that can no longer distinguish between right and wrong—that in fact denies that any such distinction can legitimately be made. Paradoxical as it may seem, it was not the theologians he disciplined who were the real dissidents—though they rejoiced in the title—but the rather shy, not very robust German who dared to say to them and to the rest of the world: Sorry, but you are wrong.

Despite all the public vilification over the past quarter of a century, Joseph Ratzinger retained his inner peace, his gentle wit, and his sharp mind. One German commentator remarked: "[U]nlike many of my compatriots, the pope is unflaggingly courteous and appears to grow even gentler in the midst of debate, though he'd never relinquish so much as an inch of ground."[31] Perhaps it is not too much to say that he bore his fate with heroic fortitude and exemplary patience. He never tried to defend himself—though he did defend the teachings he espoused and was not afraid manfully to enter into public dialogue with those who criticized him or held contrary views. Over the thirty-five years that I have known him, an ever deeper inner calm seems to

---

[31] Mosebach, *International Herald Tribune* (May 3, 2005), continues: "His enemies called him cold because he refuses to feign cordiality. And it is true: His manner shows nothing of the effusive Dale Carnegie mould so admired in Germany. However, he is not 'cold' as a person. He simply retains his personal distance from the objectivity of the truth he articulates and defends."

have settled on him, while his confidence has grown, not in his own ability, but in the truth he perceives, admittedly as in a glass darkly (see 1 Cor 13:12), the truth that humanity needs more than anything else if it is to attain fulfillment and happiness.

One of the central concepts of Ratzinger's theology is that of *Stellvertretung*, representation or substitution—in particular, the substitution of the innocent for the guilty, such as the Suffering Servant of Deutero-Isaiah and, preeminently, the suffering of the Innocent One on the Cross for the salvation of guilty mankind, when Jesus, who knew not sin, became sin for our sakes (see 2 Cor 5:21). This, according to Ratzinger, is the principle of Christian existence. Few outside (or even inside) Germany know about the contemplative nuns who, whether in the shadow of the concentration camp at Dachau or near the place of execution at Plötzensee, Berlin, have consecrated their lives to God in reparation for the crimes of their fellow countrymen. They live lives of true *Stellvertretung*. They and more than 354 German Catholic martyrs[32] who perished at the hands of the Nazis have, in Christ, helped to wash away the stain of the nation's guilt.

Together with the millions of other innocent Germans after the war, Ratzinger, too, silently bore the guilt of his people and so helped redeem them from the ignominy of the recent past. After he was elected pope, his countryman Cardinal Karl Lehmann, President of the German Bishops' Conference, who did not always see eye-to-eye with Ratzinger, announced that the Second World War was finally over: Germany could once again take its rightful place among the nations of the world.

[32] A list of the Protestant martyrs has not yet been compiled.

But, of course, the election of the man whom the media had portrayed as the Grand Inquisitor to succeed the popular Pope John Paul II has, perhaps, a more theological significance. Ratzinger stood for the uncompromising truth that is of divine origin, not of man's fashioning. He suffered for it, and he persevered in his witness to it irrespective of a negative media image, indeed intense hostility. For him, Christian existence is precisely that: life lived for others, life as a service to others, where we bear each other's burdens, where the innocent suffer for the guilty—in and with Christ. "To be a Christian", he wrote, "is an appeal to a person's magnanimity, to his high-mindedness, that he is ready with Simon of Cyrene to bear the world-historical Cross of Jesus Christ, the weight of the whole of history, and so serve the true life." [33] The innocent one, the Christian, gives his life "for the many". All his teaching as a theology professor, his entire ministry as a bishop and cardinal prefect had but one objective: to serve that truth which humanity needs more than food and water, the truth that "God is love", the theme of his first encyclical.

Joseph Ratzinger is now Vicar of Christ on earth: "Vicar" is another word for *Stellvertreter* (the representative). Benedict XVI, the German pope—more precisely, the European pope—is now called by God to serve the whole of mankind, that all may come to know Christ Jesus, the truth that alone can make us free. He is called to give the final years of his full life for the sake of the many. Europe's

---

[33] Cf. his article "Stellvertretung", in *Handbuch theologischer Grundbegriffe*, vol. 4 (Munich: Kösel, 1970), p. 136. For an excellent account of the theology of *Stellvertretung*, see Lore Bartholomäus, *Studien zum Leidensproblem in der Erziehung: Theologische Grundfragen einer Pädogogik der Leidbewältigung* (Frankfurt am Main: Fischer, 1981), pp. 115–207.

legacy to the world has been as ambiguous as Germany's legacy to Europe. As a European pope, Benedict XVI, one may hope, will help undo some of the damage done by European colonialism and the negative effects of the Enlightenment on the rest of the world. He will do so as the conscience of our age.

Chapter Seven

THE FUTURE UNDER
POPE BENEDICT XVI

Many did not greet the election of Joseph Cardinal Ratzinger with elation. Some were disappointed that someone more "liberal" had not been elected. Others were influenced by his negative public image, thanks to his former position as the Church's official "no-sayer". This response often dismayed those who knew him either personally or through his numerous publications. Based on his negative image, many fear for the future of the Church. But those who know him think otherwise. I wish to offer some comments on the kind of future I think we can look forward to during the pontificate of Pope Benedict XVI.

His surprise choice of the name Benedict gives us an important clue as to what his priorities will be and what our hope for the future should be, fully aware that man proposes but God disposes. His predecessor Benedict XV came to the office of Peter with an image not dissimilar to that of Cardinal Ratzinger before his election, but he turned out to be a reconciling pope, helping to overcome theological divisions within the Church and reaching out to the

Eastern Churches. As Pope Benedict XVI hinted in his first homily as pope, he will promote dialogue, dialogue within the Church to help heal the real divisions there, dialogue with fellow Christians separated from us, and dialogue with the non-Christian religions. Secondly, in a world overshadowed by wars and terrorism, he will work toward peace and reconciliation, as his predecessor worked for peace among nations during World War I.

Benedict is the name of one of the great founders of Western monasticism (ca. 480–ca. 550), whose profound influence during the following centuries earned him the title of Father of Western Civilization. In their deliberations leading up to the conclave, during which they discussed the state of the Church in the world today, the cardinals may have argued somewhat as follows: The Church in Latin America, Africa, and Asia are flourishing. They might need encouragement and material help. Europe needs renewal and spiritual help. It needs to recover its soul. The Churches in Europe are the sick members of the Body of Christ. While the Church in other continents is flourishing—despite enormous problems at the social and economic levels—the materially rich West is spiritually and culturally imploding.

The West not only exports technology and goods (often undermining the economies and social fabric of what we call, somewhat derogatorily, the "Third World"). It also exports ideas and ideologies, such as liberal capitalism and Marxism, both of which are rooted in cultural developments that are uniquely European. More generally and more perniciously, European thinkers have also emitted the poisonous gas of the "hermeneutics of suspicion" into the cultural environment—including the distrust of all traditions and authority—which is the cause of Europe's spiritual crisis and which we have already spread to other continents. Those ideas have fostered a radical questioning of every aspect of human tradition with an inner logic that in time can only undermine all of man's wisdom traditions. These ideas have fostered doubt rather than trust as the first movement of the human mind. Exported to Asia and Africa, these ideas threaten indigenous cultural and religious traditions more than any technological or social change. They undermine human flourishing. As the Holy Father highlighted in his sermon during his Inauguration Mass: "The external deserts in the world are growing, because the internal deserts have become so vast." The sickness of the Churches in Europe must be healed before it does any more damage to the rest of the Body of Christ.

The cardinals in conclave also knew that, despite appearances, there is a springtime of faith in the European Churches. The countless young people attending World Youth Days, mourning Pope John Paul II, and greeting his newly elected successor testify to this. The conclave, it would seem, wanted to promote this new springtime by electing Joseph Ratzinger as pope. And he will further its growth, as already indicated by his impressive performance in Cologne during the World Youth Day 2005.

Recovery of the Christian roots of Europe is the only remedy for Europe's spiritual sickness. These roots are found, not simply in Scripture and tradition, but also in the classical Greek philosophical and Roman jurisprudential traditions, which were taken up into European Christian culture to the mutual enrichment of both. Pope John Paul II called for a reevangelization of Europe, which to date has largely fallen on deaf ears, not least, it seems, because of Europe's pride at being "advanced", "developed", and "progressive"—and thus not really in need of anything. We once sent missionaries to other continents, but we are not truly convinced that now our own continent urgently needs to be reevangelized. In this corner of the globe (and here we must include North America), we often assume that we (advanced, progressive people) know what is best for the rest of the world. We also seem to be increasingly incapable of constructive self-criticism.

Some commentators expressed the fear that the election of Benedict XVI would drive people out of the Church. However, to date those who were—to put it mildly—least enthusiastic at his election have simply announced that they would wait and see how he performs. The only people who might leave the Church as a result of what the Pope says are those who do not share his poverty of spirit, his humility, and his ability to engage in self-criticism. Most ordinary people—who intuitively grasp truths that great thinkers articulate in words and in art—will respond positively to the Pope's retiring personality and enlightening discourse, since they recognize with surprise and joy the truths already vaguely familiar to them but now articulated with a clarity that is illuminating.

After the winter of the twentieth century, when Europe cast a shadow of fear over the face of the earth, and Germany in particular terrorized it twice, the Churches of Europe and America under the inspiration of the German pope will, I am convinced, undergo a rebirth. Having regained their spiritual youth again, they will become worthy to join the company of the young, vibrant Churches of Latin America, Africa, and Asia. His writings will sow the seeds of truth, which in time will bear spiritual fruit in abundance.

Ratzinger's whole life has been a preparation for his papacy. His earliest formation was rooted in the study of the ancient classics and the best of European literature, while his philosophical and theological training introduced him, not only to the breadth and depth of the Latin and Greek theological traditions, but also to the Enlightenment tradition that marks modern Europe and America in particular. As we saw in chapter 1, the breadth of subjects covered by Ratzinger in his writings and the profundity of his thought on issues as diverse as bioethics, Christology, politics, non-Christian religions, and ecumenism are astonishing. He can, literally, talk on any subject off the cuff, and do so in a way that is clear, concise, and beautifully crafted. He will listen to others, as he always did as a professor or as a conversationalist; he will discern wisely; and, where possible, he will try to open up new horizons.

The name Benedict may also suggest that the reform of the liturgy will be a priority, because the Benedictine tradition has long been associated with liturgical excellence. The Pope is a lover of music, in particular of Mozart, and art. He was brought up in the Baroque tradition of rich liturgies. As cardinal prefect, Ratzinger was concerned about the way the liturgy had been impoverished by well-meaning attempts to reform it. And so he wrote extensively on the subject of the liturgy attempting to recover the true "spirit of the liturgy", focused on worship and the mystery of God's presence in human words, actions, bread, and wine.

The faith of ordinary Catholics has been shattered by many developments in the Church, not least in the way the liturgy is celebrated. Ratzinger knows that tradition is a living thing. The past cannot be simply "restored" (like some old building) as though nothing had happened in the meantime. Restoration, as advocated by Ratzinger, must of necessity be creative, rooted in theology, and concerned with the essentials, not the accidentals. Our task instead is to allow a new form of liturgy to emerge organically under the guidance of sound theological principles tested in tradition. It should be a form of liturgy that is at the same time "familiar", a liturgy where people feel at home and yet long for that Home beyond. But it must be a liturgy that, though it transcends all cultures, yet echoes each people's own culture. Finally, it must be a spiritual liturgy, one that will provide the hope and inspiration we all need in the rough and tumble of everyday life.

As noted above, Ratzinger wrote extensively on the theology of political life in modern Europe, a theology not uninfluenced by his own experience and by his rejection of both totalitarianism and consumerism, each of which in its own way leads to the death of the spirit. He is aware of the danger to a society where there is no moral consensus—or only a deficient one. He will try to persuade European people, believers or not, that we can discover objective criteria for right and wrong, which will give law its foundation and provide democracy with the moral framework that is indispensable to its functioning as democracy. Like Václav Havel, Ratzinger, too, is critical of the effect of such moral relativism on Western political life and well being, where might becomes right, politics becomes manipulation, and propaganda replaces debate. Ratzinger calls for the renewal of political life based on the principle of personal responsibility: conscience. The world can look forward to an exciting future under Pope Benedict XVI.

Epilogue

A QUESTION OF FAIRNESS: CRITIQUE OF A BIOGRAPHY

Cardinal Ratzinger as Prefect of the Congregation for the Doctrine of the Faith was perhaps the most controversial figure in the Church up to his election as Pope Benedict XVI. Indeed, for many he is still a rather dubious character. He is, in fact, himself a subject awaiting an author. Various articles about him have appeared in sundry magazines, but, up to 2003, there was no book devoted to his life, no book, that is, until the appearance of one by the Vatican correspondent for the *National Catholic Reporter*, John L. Allen, Jr.* This book is a strange mixture, part

* *Cardinal Ratzinger: The Vatican's Enforcer of the Faith*, by John L. Allen, Jr. (New York and London: Continuum, 2000). After Ratzinger's election as pope, the book was reprinted in America "for obvious reasons" (Allen), though without consulting the author, as: *Pope Benedict XVI: A Biography of Joseph Ratzinger*. The British publishers asked Allen to write a preface, "so at least the damage will be limited in the U.K.", as the author put it. Allen (in "The Word from Rome", *NCR*, April 26, 2005) had been rather shaken by criticisms of his book by Father Joseph Komonchak and admits that "If I were to write the book again today, I'm sure it would be more balanced, better informed, and less prone to veer off into judgment ahead of sober analysis." In the aftermath of Ratzinger's election as pope, Allen produced in record

early biography (chaps. 1–3), part chronicle of some major controversies (chaps. 4–6), part judgment on Cardinal Joseph Ratzinger's performance as "enforcer of the faith" and his chances at becoming future pope (chaps. 7–8). It was also a strange experience for me to read a book about someone I know personally (and have revered) for over thirty years and yet not really recognize either the person or the theologian I know described in it. Even though he spent "more than a year of [his] life listening—listening *hard*—to Ratzinger" (p. 304), the author seems to have had some difficulty "hearing" the Prefect of the Congregation for the Doctrine of the Faith. More seriously, one may ask, is Allen fair to Ratzinger? Is this a reliable account of such an important churchman?

Toward the end of the book, Allen describes the Cardinal as "in most ways the best and brightest the Catholic Church of his generation has to offer, a musician and man of culture, a genteel intellectual and polyglot, a deep true believer" (p. 313). Yet, Allen adds, he has left in his wake a fractured Church. The "yet" (or its equivalent) well typifies Allen's account of Ratzinger's position on various theological and ecclesiastical issues. Allen generally presents a concise account, though lacking any great depth or insight,

time a short volume: *The Rise of Benedict XVI: The Inside Story of How the Pope was Elected and What It Means for the World* (London: Penguin Books, 2005), which indeed lives up to these standards. It is clear that Allen now has a better understanding of both the man and his thought. Chapter 5 is a biography of Joseph Ratzinger, concise and, as far as I can judge, accurate. (He corrected at least two errors of fact that I pointed out in my review article.) However, since it is still the most comprehensive biography available, I have decided to reprint an annotated and somewhat expanded version of this review that first appeared in "A Question of Fairness", *Homiletic & Pastoral Review* 102/1 (2001): 53–57.

before going on to cancel the positive statement by some perceived "fault" or other. In his concluding chapter, he also offers his readers a succinct summary of the main points of what he considers to be of enduring value in what he read by Ratzinger over the period of a year (pp. 303–6). Anyone skeptical of Allen might first read this to be assured of his good faith. So too, Allen's accounts of various major controversies, in particular the chapter on liberation theology, are invariably interesting. How accurate they are is another matter, but the author generally *tries* to be fair and balanced. The crucial question is: To what extent does he succeed?

In the final analysis, the Cardinal remains, for Allen, the bogeyman who frightens most liberals, the main source of division and demoralization in the contemporary Church, the one whose later theological views, in contrast with his earlier "liberal" stance, have had the effect, *inter alia*, of "legitimising the concentration of power in the hands of the pope and his immediate advisors in the Roman curia" (p. 309). In other words, despite all his efforts to be fair, and Allen does make considerable efforts in that direction, the Cardinal remains the ogre. Take, for example, Allen's account of the liberation theology saga culminating in its effective defeat in large measure due to Ratzinger's theological analysis and, more importantly, it is claimed, his ecclesiastical, political machinations. This account is not without its merits, but one's confidence in Allen's historical judgment is placed under severe strain when he blames the Cardinal for the failure of Latin American Catholicism to create a social order that better reflects gospel values, namely, less inequality between rich and poor (see p. 173). One could reasonably argue that more might have been accomplished at the political level in Latin America if liberation theologians, at the outset, had not been so skeptical of both Catholic social teaching and the potential of indigenous cultural traditions of piety, which they later rediscovered, to effect political change, but that is another issue.

Allen claims that Ratzinger's attitude to other religions is negative, yet he fails to note, for example, that the Patriarch of Constantinople awarded the then Professor Ratzinger the Golden Cross of Mount Athos for his contribution to a greater understanding between Catholicism and Orthodoxy. Later on, as Cardinal, he joined his former students at the Orthodox center near Geneva for a most amicable and fruitful discussion with representatives of the Greek Orthodox Church, whose tradition he frequently cites. Allen seems not to know anything about the Cardinal's role in helping to establish diplomatic relations between the Vatican and Israel. And not a word is heard of his defense of Islam from the blanket charge of fundamentalism[1] or his appreciation of the significance of primordial religious rituals and myths, as found, for example, in the Hindu tradition.[2]

More serious is Allen's sweeping allegation that: "Like Ratzinger's crusades against liberation theology, feminism, and gay rights, the pall he has cast over ecumenism and interreligious dialogue has had consequences beyond the borders of academic theology. It has contributed to making the world a more fractured, and therefore a more dangerous place." In other words, Cardinal Ratzinger's supposedly negative attitude to the other religions must necessarily exacerbate religious conflict in the world. This

[1] Cf. *TPE* 165–70.
[2] See, for example, Joseph Cardinal Ratzinger, "Eucharist and Mission", *Irish Theological Quarterly* 65/3 (2000): 257.

really is nonsense. Northern Ireland is specifically mentioned among a list of conflicts around the world with a religious dimension, but anyone close to the scene knows that, at least on the Catholic side, religion was and is not an issue. When *Dominus Iesus* was published, the then Anglican Archbishop of Armagh, Ireland, did indeed make a claim similar to that of Allen's. A wry smile was the general reaction, even from those unsympathetic to the content of the declaration.

But it is above all in Allen's attempt to write a life of Cardinal Ratzinger (chaps. 1–3) that the distorting effect of what seems to be the liberal's underlying fear of the bogeyman can be seen. The main goal in these opening chapters, it would appear, is to find an explanation for the transmutation into the "enforcer of the faith" of the earlier "liberal" Ratzinger, the young and promising theologian, who as peritus to Cardinal Frings played such an important role at the Second Vatican Council.

Joseph Ratzinger grew up in the shadow of Nazi Germany within a family that was decidedly anti-Nazi and a Church that was intensely hostile to Hitler[3]—though, of course, perhaps not as publicly defiant as a later generation that did not live in those circumstances might claim it should have been. That experience undoubtedly had an influence on Ratzinger, as he himself has expressly said. But the claim that "Ratzinger today believes that the best antidote to political totalitarianism is ecclesial totalitarianism" (p. 3)—however appealing as a sound bite—does not stand up to

---

[3] Apart from references to the Germany of his youth and the Church in Bavaria that formed his piety in *MM* and *SE*, see the interview with Cardinal Ratzinger conducted by Robert Moynihan in 1993 (note 21, p. 145 above) for the most comprehensive account of his youth and his experiences during the war, a rich source for future biographers.

scrutiny.[4] It is, however, the *leitmotif* of the whole book. On the contrary, according to Cardinal Ratzinger himself, the best antidote to totalitarianism is the upright conscience typically associated with the poor and the weak.[5] And the role of the Church, already mentioned, is primarily educational—understood in the spirit of the Greek philosophers—namely, "to break open the prison of positivism and awaken man's receptivity to the truth, to God, and thus to the power of conscience".[6] The primacy of conscience, though of central importance to Cardinal Ratzinger, both as a man and as a theologian, is not even mentioned by Allen.

More serious are the insinuations about the "failure" of Ratzinger's own family to show more overt opposition to the Nazi terror. Such a judgment shows little understanding of what living in a reign of terror involves, especially for a policeman and his young family (one is reminded of the film *La vita è bella*).[7] Unaware of other autobiographical references to that time, Allen fails to note the context of Ratzinger's few and scattered remarks about his childhood, which were not intended to be either detailed or exhaustive. And he seems to be unaware of other occasions

[4] Asked by Moynihan about what influence the Nazi period had had on him, Ratzinger replied: "In two ways, I would say. First, we were made more aware of our faith.... And then second, I would say that we saw a certain anti-Christian vision of the world that, in the final analysis, showed itself to be anti-human and absurd, [though], at first, being in power, it displayed itself as the great hope of humanity. And as a result, I learned to have a certain reserve with regard to the reigning ideologies" (ibid., p. 41).

[5] Cf. *Internationale katholische Zeitschrift Communio* I (1972): 432–42; also in *Reinhold Schneider Gesellschaft e.V.*, Heft 4, July 1972, pp. 13–19; reprinted in *CEP* 165–80.

[6] *TPE* 55, not mentioned in Allen's brief bibliography. See also his *CPE* 263 and 254.

[7] See Ratzinger's comments on his father above, pp. 146f.

when Ratzinger spoke of that period, such as his recollection of how in 1941 it became obvious to everyone that
there was something sinister behind the disappearance of
five neighbors, one, a cousin with Down's Syndrome. It
was in fact the liquidation of the "unproductive" by the
Nazis. In this context, he also mentions the relief everyone
felt when Cardinal von Galen had the courage to protest.[8]

Allen claims that Ratzinger tends to be selective in his
own memory of those times. To prove that Ratzinger's positive appraisal of the role of the Catholic Church at the
time was "one-sided and even distorted in its emphasis on
the moral courage of the church, at the expense of an hon-
est reckoning with its failures" (p. 30), Allen claims that
"Hitler came to power on the back of Catholic support"
(p. 27). This is a serious misinterpretation of events.[9] Allen
gives no source for this or similar doubtful interpretations
of events. Indeed, his failure to give his sources is a major
weakness of the book.[10] It would seem that here Allen is
following some very biased reading of the historical events.
But the reader is left with the vague, overall impression
that Cardinal Ratzinger must be hiding something. And so,
a shadow is cast over his youth in preparation for the emergence of the full-blown ogre in later life.

It is a cliché in popular theological circles to distinguish between the early and the late Ratzinger. He himself

[8] Cf. Cardinal Joseph Ratzinger "The Likeness of God in the Human
Being", *Dolentium Hominum*, no. 34 (1997): 17. (Allen used this piece of
information in his 2005 book on Benedict XVI, where he gives a more
balanced picture of the Nazi period in Ratzinger's life.)

[9] See above, chap. 6.

[10] There are only 120 footnotes for 314 pages of text, a number of which
are references to articles in the *National Catholic Reporter*. This does not inspire
confidence.

maintains that, though there are changes (mostly of emphasis), there is also a basic continuity in his theology, a continuity that is not inconsistent with significant changes in
perspective, even at times contradicting isolated claims he
made in his theological youth. He himself points to a significant development in his eschatology. After all, "to live
is to change." Is it too much to suggest that the changes
in his thinking might best be interpreted as signs of matu-
rity, of further reflection due to changing circumstances
and broader experience, especially as Prefect of the Congregation? His youthful enthusiasm for collegiality, for example, gave way to a reappraisal of the institution of national
episcopal conferences in the light of his own personal experience in such conferences and as a result of his further
theological reflection. He also noted the failure of the German bishops during the Nazi period to act more deci-
sively and effectively because of the tendency of any group
acting collectively to find the lowest common denominator.

Instead, Allen attributes a radical change from "erstwhile
liberal" to the conservative "enforcer of the faith" to four
causes: the 1968 student unrest, perceptions of decline in
church attendance and vocations, too much exposure to
Catholic faith at its most distorted, and, finally, power. The
student unrest in the late 1960s did have a profound effect
on anyone who lived through that turbulent period, and
the Cardinal himself has on occasion referred to this, though
it seems to me that his reflections on this period make use
of ideas he had already formed in his earlier writings. But
it is doubtful if the decline in church numbers could have
had such a radical effect on him. At a discussion of precisely this topic during a meeting of his former students,
he once remarked that the sin for which David was most
severely punished by the Lord was not his adultery or the

murder of Bethsheba's husband, but the census, the king's attempt to number the people of God. Thirdly, his exposure as prefect to the "pathology of the faith", as Allen calls it, would seem to be offset by his own wide reading in the Fathers, contemporary theology, and philosophy, not to mention literature. His scholarly disposition to read and research finds due expression in various scholarly and general publications. And so one is left with the final "cause": power. To suggest that the lust for power played a central role in any supposed "change of heart", that Professor Ratzinger revised his theology to advance his career, is absurd, if not tantamount to calumny.[11] As mentioned above, Ratzinger's chief characteristic as a man and as a theologian is that he does not take himself that seriously. What he does take seriously is his quest for the truth.

His so-called "change of heart" in theology, it is claimed, is reflected in the two *Schülerkreise* (not *Studentenkreise*, the term Allen uses) he is supposed to have built up: those from his years in Bonn, Münster, and Tübingen and those from his years in Regensburg, "the latter group theologically at odds with the former" (p. 104). This division "underlines the gap between Ratzinger before and after the Council". I am mentioned as an example of the latter group. Allen seems to have conducted fairly extensive interviews with two students of the "earlier Ratzinger" (Verweyen and Böckenförde), but only

---

[11] The author fails to recognize the status of a university professor (*Ordinarius*) in Germany, which is generally regarded as higher than that of a bishop. At the time he was made Archbishop of Munich, against his will (a fact for which I can personally vouch), he was at his most creative and productive as a writer and a lecturer, the activities he most enjoys. Thus his acceptance of the See of Munich was at the cost of considerable personal sacrifice, tempered only by the opportunity it offered him to serve his own native diocese in his beloved Bavaria.

spoke briefly on the "phone to one of the 'later Ratzinger'", Father Joseph Fessio, S.J., who in fact spent a rela-
tively short time in Regensburg. Considering the number of
postgraduate students who studied under Ratzinger (somewhere between forty and fifty), this is slim evidence on which
to base such a far-reaching thesis. Allen is wrong on several
details, such as describing me as a spokesman for the Archbishop of Dublin (untrue) and citing extracts from my writings, especially from my thesis, without any regard for the
context. More seriously, he erroneously makes Cardinal
Schönborn a student of Ratzinger's, devoting several pages to
the present Archbishop of Vienna to illustrate the "later
Ratzinger".[12]

It is, further, misleading to say that Ratzinger "built up"
two distinct circles of students. There was never more than
one, though its composition obviously changed with its
members.[13] Indeed, some of his students from his time in
Bonn, Münster, and Tübingen might well be considered to
number among his more "conservative" students, while others who started their studies while he was in Regensburg

[12] Schönborn, indeed, spent one academic year in Regensburg, while con-
ducting research on his book *L'Icône de Christ* (Fribourg: Éditions Universi-
taires, 1976). During that time, he joined Ratzinger's doctoral colloquium,
as was the custom with other visiting scholars. But he was not a student of
Ratzinger as such, though he became a permanent guest, like Franz Muss-
ner, Emeritus Professor of the New Testament, when the doctoral colloquium was transformed into the annual meeting of Ratzinger's former students
after his election as Archbishop of Munich and so is listed among his students. (Allen corrected this error in his 2005 book on Benedict XVI.)

[13] For a detailed description of Ratzinger's *Schülerkreis* and its activities,
see the article by his former assistant, Professor Stephan Otto Horn, S.D.S.,
"Il Cardinale Ratzinger e i suoi studenti", in Josef Clemens and Antonio
Tarzia, eds., *Alla scuola della Verità: I settanta anni di Joseph Ratzinger* (Cinisello
Balsamo: San Paolo, 1997), pp. 9–26. Regretfully, Allen was apparently unaware
of this invaluable source.

are held to be among his more "liberal" students. However, it is true to say that his critical views on postconciliar developments did tend to attract students more sympathetic to such views. More significant is the fact that all students, irrespective of their basic standpoint, felt at home in the colloquium. This is because of Ratzinger's evident respect for each one, his quite remarkable ability to promote dialogue and discussion, and his tolerance of diverse viewpoints. I have attended many a seminar on and off the university campus, but I have never encountered a teacher who could engender such a free and frank discussion as Professor Ratzinger could. His readiness to give his students total academic freedom in their choice and treatment of topic was also remarkable.

It is therefore simply untrue to claim that it was at Regensburg "that Ratzinger began educating a generation of students who would go on to play a leading restoration role in their own national churches" (p. 92). He never set out to indoctrinate any group of students, as seems to be implied here. The seminars and colloquia in Regensburg were places of intense debate and disagreement—and of wit and humor, it should be added. This was also a time of intensive ecumenical activities, including his pioneering lecture on the future of ecumenism at the University of Graz in 1976,[14] his participation at the Regensburg Ecumenical Symposia, and the end-of-the-year, extended doctoral colloquia with the Lutheran theologians Pannenberg and Joest, none of which Allen mentions. What Professor Ratzinger taught us at Regensburg, primarily by his example, was to search for the truth with scholarly rigor, to be objective and

---

[14] Cf. Joseph Ratzinger, "Prognosen für die Zukunft des Ökumenismus", in *Ökumenisches Forum: Grazer Helfte für konkrete Ökumene* 1 (1978): 31–41.

respectful in debate, to risk unpopularity if necessary, and above all to give reasons for one's convictions. Occasionally, the reproach was even heard that he had failed to form his own distinct "school", so diverse were his students and so open was the atmosphere he cultivated. In this, he has not changed with the years, as evidenced by the yearly meeting with his former students. He once remarked that he had learned much from his students. It would be a wild exaggeration to say that he was as much influenced by us as we were formed by him, but it would not be without some basis in fact.

This characteristic of openness and dialogue is perhaps the key to understanding Ratzinger then and now: it is expressive of his concern for truth, which, he is convinced, will always prevail in the end (cf. p. 286), and explains both the primacy of conscience and the role of the Church in his writings. This in turn involves the greatest possible objectivity, or rather the continual (personal and collective) search for what is in fact true, and, so, openness to the opinions of others, openness to change, and the courage to speak the truth in love. As a result, Ratzinger manages to preserve a certain distance from all the controversies that embroil him and his office. Contrary to what is claimed in this book, he *is* ready to listen.

Consistent with this thinking is the statement in the *Instruction on the Ecclesial Vocation of the Theologian* that a judgment of the Church on theological writings "does not concern the *person* of the theologian but the *intellectual positions* which he has publicly espoused" (my emphasis). For this reason, it is strange for Allen to claim that when "Ratzinger denounces a theologian, he also implicitly rejects his theology" (p. 242). On the contrary, he, as prefect, disciplined theologians because of their theology, not the other way around, and could only do so if they were recalcitrant in their refusal to accept the authoritative judgment of the Church. For Allen to underline the personal charm of Charles Curran, whom "virtually no one who knows him could construe as an enemy of the faith" (p. 258), is to miss the point completely.

In passing judgment on the "enforcer of the faith"—itself a loaded term coined by our author—Allen fails to appreciate the extent to which the Cardinal Prefect has in fact made the Congregation for the Doctrine of the Faith conform in letter and spirit to the reform inaugurated by Pope Paul VI. This was symbolized most recently when Cardinal Ratzinger opened the archives of the Congregation to scholarly research (not mentioned by Allen). It is also evident in the way he takes considerable pains to give the reasons for each decision taken by the Congregation. Few of his predecessors have provided anything like the close argumentation to be found in documents such as *Donum Vitae* or the two *Instructions on Liberation Theology*. Though on two occasions Allen quotes from papers read by Ratzinger to meetings held between officers of his Congregation and presidents of episcopal doctrinal commissions on various continents, he misses the real import of such meetings. They were attempts to enter into dialogue with the Churches in Asia, Africa, Europe, and America, to bring the center to the periphery, as it were, to listen, to promote debate. That Ratzinger did listen was clear to us when, at the annual meeting of his *Schülerkreis*, he spoke informally about various events of the previous year involving his Congregation. I got the distinct impression, for example, that, while in Zaire, he appreciated the adaptation of the Mass to African culture, including the incorporation of ritual dance in that particular liturgy. Apart from the seminars on papal primacy, Allen seems unaware of various other seminars organized by the Congregation under Ratzinger's direction to listen to and learn from experts from around the world on controversial questions, for example, in moral theology and bioethics. Neither is there any mention of the publication by the Pontifical Biblical Commission (under his direction) of the important document *The Interpretation of the Bible in the Church* (1993). In addition, Cardinal Ratzinger has continued to lecture and publish in his own name as a theologian, inviting criticism.[15] That he listens and responds to serious objections is illustrated by his readiness to enter into public debate, as in his extensive interview (covering two full pages) with the *Frankfurter Allgemeine Zeitung* (September 22, 2000) on hostile reactions to *Dominus Iesus*.

Finally, far from trying to centralize power in Rome, he has been heard to complain that, because the local bishops fail to act (or feel powerless to act when faced with a theologian who has built up his own international network), his Congregation is often reluctantly drawn into the controversy. Allen's account of the case of Father Tissa Balasuriya would have been more credible if Allen had taken the trouble to investigate the way this particular case ended up in Rome.

Allen describes a book quoted by Ratzinger (in a discussion of the pluralist theology of religions) as being reputed to be "tendentious and error-prone, down to small details such as citing the wrong page" (p. 240, again no source is given for this serious accusation). This is really the kettle calling the pot black. As I have briefly described, Allen's book is error-prone, down to small details of German spelling. It is

---

[15] From the scant bibliography given by Allen, one could be forgiven for thinking, falsely, that Ratzinger's publications were very limited. For the most complete bibliography of Ratinger's publications up to 2001, see the introduction above, n. 6.

certainly tendentious. This is illustrated not only by its sub-title but above all by the uncritical way Allen quotes accusations made by hostile witnesses, such as Hans Küng, without ever questioning their objectivity or veracity. And, apart from those gaps already mentioned, there are other serious lacunae. There is, for example, no appreciation of Ratzinger's writings in areas such as spirituality, politics, and ethics. Many of his sermons, meditations, and retreat talks have been published, even in English, but his spirituality does not merit Allen's attention. Neither is there any treatment of his substantial body of writings on politics and ethics.[16] International recognition of his unique contribution to the field of politics and ethics came when he was appointed a "membre associé étranger" at the Académie des Sciences Morales et Politiques of the Institut de France on November 7, 1992, in Paris, taking the seat vacated by the death of the Soviet dissident Andrey Sakharov. One searches in vain for any reference to this significant fact in Allen's book.

Allen is neither a theologian nor a historian. He is a journalist, who, to his credit, is aware of the particular stable from which he comes (as a correspondent for the *National Catholic Reporter*). The strength of his journalistic approach is his ability to write a narrative that, for the most part at least, keeps one's attention, though this reader began to tire of the underlying tendentiousness halfway through the book. Despite the book's drawbacks, Allen gives the reader, who otherwise might not even glance at any of Cardinal Ratzinger's writings, a little taste of the richness to be found

---

[16] For an introduction to Ratzinger's theology of politics, see Vincent Twomey, "Zur Theologie des Politischen", in *Joseph Kardinal Ratzinger: Von Wiederauffinden der Mitte: Grundorientierung; Texte aus vier Jahrzehnten*, ed. Stephan Otto Horn, S.D.S., et al. (Freiburg im Breisgau: Herder, 1997; 2nd printing 1998), pp. 219–30.

therein, and he conveys something of the importance of this largely underestimated theologian holding one of the central offices in the Church at this tempestuous yet exhilarating time in history. But the price to be paid is a rather black-and-white approach to a man who is far more subtle, charming, and courageous than the one portrayed here, a man whose theology is not "derivative", as some anonymous theologian quoted by Allen claims, but highly original and seminal, covering a vast range of subjects with refreshing clarity and insight. Though this book is not fair to Cardinal Ratzinger, its publication may prompt others to study his original writings, to judge for themselves—and so to enter into dialogue with one of the truly great thinkers of our age.

Appendix 2

SERMON BY POPE BENEDICT XVI
IN CASTEL GANDOLFO
FOR THE MEMBERS OF HIS
SCHÜLERKREIS
ON SEPTEMBER 4, 2005
(Twenty-third Sunday in Year 1)

Ezekiel 33:7–9
Romans 13: 8–10
Matthew 18:15–20

Dear Friends,

The Gospel we have just heard consists quite clearly of three fragments, which, at first sight, appear to be only loosely connected with each other. To begin with, there is an initial piece of canon law, one might say, showing an incipient Church order or Church disciplinary procedure, as people like to say nowadays. Then follows the granting of the power to bind and loose, which two chapters earlier had been given to Peter, but now is given to the Church as a whole, and finally we hear the words of promise about prayer being answered. If we look more closely, we shall see that these apparently somewhat unrelated fragments are in fact closely interconnected

Translated by Martin Henry.

and can be properly understood only if taken together. Those responsible for the liturgy have likewise succeeded in selecting two other readings that also are in inner harmony with today's Gospel and help us to understand it better.

To begin with, what we have here is an early form of Church order. What is obvious is that, even as she begins to grow, the early Church, which aims to be, and ought to be, the perfect community of love, is in need of order and of law. The order that is outlined here resembles somewhat that of Qumran, but also that of the Synagogue. In any case, the point is that, on the one hand, there must be discretion, love of the neighbor, and respect for the neighbor, while, on the other hand—and at the same time—the neighbor must be reprimanded, so that he can find his way back into the order of love, which he has abandoned, even to the extent of incurring excommunication. Naturally, the question immediately arises: Is it really in the spirit of Jesus to speak of punishment that includes excommunication? Is that compatible with the preceding parable of the shepherd, who goes in search of the lost sheep, wherever it has strayed, takes it on his shoulders, and brings it home? Is it compatible with the previous mention of continual forgiveness? Indeed it is; in fact, continual forgiveness is only possible within such a Church order. The way law and love are intertwined in this context can best be understood in the light of the two other readings in today's Mass. Paul, in the second reading, tells us that love encompasses the entire law—and that includes justice in its *entirety*. To say that love does not harm the neighbor means at the same time that justice can be a form of love. It also means that at times love requires justice to be done, so that the neighbor can again be brought back to the right path and can find his way back to the path of love that he has abandoned.

The excerpt from the Prophet Ezekiel's words to the shepherds, which was the first reading for today's Mass, may help us even more. There we find an urgent appeal to the shepherds to warn the neighbor who goes astray; if the shepherd fails to do so, he will himself have a share of the blame for what happens. Saint Augustine, a man with a great desire for peace and harmony, and who on that account found it difficult as a pastor to have to keep pestering his flock and applying the law to them as well, never ceased to reflect and ponder on these words of Ezekiel to the shepherds. In his sermons, he applied them over and over again to himself and his confreres, such as on the anniversary of his own ordination or at other episcopal ordinations. One particular comparison he used on such an occasion has remained firmly fixed in my memory. He said: I often have to pester you and to seem to be unpleasant, indeed, unkind toward you. And yet at the same time, he said, the image I have in my mind is of someone suffering from sleeping sickness. In that condition, a person is in danger of falling asleep for good, of falling into the sleep of death; he can only be saved by being constantly awakened: And he will say to whoever rouses him and wakes him up: Leave me alone, I just want to sleep, leave me in peace. He will resist whoever is importunate enough to try to wake him, when all he wants to do is sleep.

Augustine's conclusion is that, if I really love the sick person, then I cannot give in to his wishes; I cannot abandon him to what would be fatal for him. This seems to me to be a powerful metaphor for the sleep of unbelief, for our religious forgetfulness, indeed, for our sleeping sickness with regard to the living God. Modern man does not want to be bothered with God. It is so comfortable—it seems—to live without God. And yet, if we let people fall into this sleeping sickness, then they will be lost and they will destroy not only themselves but also the possibility of creating any human community. For this reason, we cannot accept this religious forgetfulness; we must become disagreeable; we must, over and over again, wrench people out of their religious forgetfulness. We have to wake them up and keep placing God—urgently and audibly—before their eyes and before their souls.

Reflecting on the Gospel in today's Mass, something of even more immediate and practical concern at the moment also occurred to me and made me see very clearly how law and love complement each another. Those of us who work in the Congregation [for the Doctrine of the Faith] were confronted with the whole tragic question of priests who were guilty of pedophilia, especially in America. The victims, their relatives, and many critical Catholics said to us: What on earth is going on in the Catholic Church? Can people do whatever they want in the Church? And we were told: All you have been concerned about is covering up for the priests. But you did not think of the victims. You only provided possibilities for the culprits to defend themselves; you exploited the possibilities provided by the law in order to ensure that nothing could ever happen to them. But you never considered the terrible damage done to others in the process. And you did not consider the common good of the Church. When the Church begins to rot from within, letting things slide in this way is destructive. With her apparent generosity and kindness, the Church is destroying the very love she seeks to foster. We were told: The way canon law is now set up, only the guilty ever enjoy its protection. You have apparently forgotten about the victims and the general Church community. The latter suffers when the guilty are allowed to go unpunished with no questions asked.

These criticisms gave us food for thought and made us once again conscious of the fact that there are three interconnected levels of goods that have to be taken into account in any human society that is genuinely concerned with law and love. Certainly, legal protection for any defendant is very important. Today's Gospel also says as much in envisaging three stages in the way a complaint should be dealt with. Legal protection for the accused means that he is not simply to be hung out to dry in the face of calumnies, insults, injustice, and insinuations. But the other two legal goods must also be kept in mind, the good of the other party, that is, the injured party, and the good of the Church as a whole. In the Church, faith and love can be destroyed by culpable behavior, particularly on the part of those who hold office. In this context it becomes clear that punishment can be the very way to awaken the sleeping conscience and, indeed, to guide someone back to the path of forgiveness who is no longer even aware of his need for forgiveness: punishment can be the way of going in search of the lost sheep, taking it on our shoulders, and bringing it back home.

To see this is of great importance for Christianity, indeed, for contemporary humanity. The "delusion of innocence", that is, the inability to recognize guilt, is a destructive sickness, a sleeping sickness of the conscience. Where, however, conscience falls asleep—we have seen it happen in the last century—man destroys both himself and the world. Hence the sleeping sickness that can affect man's conscience must not be ignored; rather his conscience must be awakened so that he can seek forgiveness. This is, in fact, an essential manifestation of love. Whereas to allow one's neighbor to become religiously forgetful or to let his conscience wither and die is to show a lack of love toward him. In other words, it is a sign of love for one's neighbor to harass him, so that he wakes up to God, so that he himself can once again become a loving person.

That brings us now to the second element in the Gospel passage for today: the power of binding and loosing. Saint Augustine has a very profound interpretation of this twofold handing over of the power to bind and loose— first to Peter and then to the Church as a whole. On the one hand, there must, he says, be a specific legal authority in the Church that is actually responsible for binding and loosing. But, on the other hand, he tells us, the specific legal authority within the Church or the person exercising this authority cannot do so in isolation or of his own accord. Rather, he can only exercise this authority because the whole Church is intrinsically involved in this act of binding and loosing. In other words, the only reason the Church can bind and loose (or punish and absolve) is because she herself also loves the sinner and because she herself also suffers with the sinner in his difficulties and his failures, just as Christ did. In this way, the sinner's failures are taken up, through the Church's suffering, into the suffering of Christ. What actually constitutes the power to loose is this willingness to suffer with and to love the sinner in his sin. The Church's love for the sinner in Christ makes the possibility of absolution a reality. The whole Church is involved in what the official Church authority is obliged to do publicly. Only through this involvement by the whole Church in the action of the official Church authority can the Church be united with the suffering and the love of Christ and, hence, united with the power that really binds and really looses, that is, with the saving power of redemption.

This brings us, finally, to the third part of this morning's Gospel reading—Christ's promise in relation to prayer. That the Church binds and looses means that she takes the difficulties and the sins of her members up into her own prayer and in this way places them in the heart of Christ. To love and suffer with the sinner in his sin means to accept the Church's discipline in a spirit of prayer. For prayer is the real power that is given to the Church. This is what today's Gospel tells us. The Lord tells us that if you pray with one mind, you will be heard. We entrust the suffering and the difficulties, the failures and the mistakes and the sins of all of us to the power of prayer—in the knowledge that we have thereby entrusted them to the heart of Christ and that we have then a share in his power to bind and loose. Yes, prayer, the strength of the Church's prayer, is where her real power to bind and loose lies; it is where her true authority lies. In prayer she is united with the Lord and hence can do here on earth things that count in heaven, too, things that count for all eternity.

Let us ask the Lord to grant us the ability to live in the Church in such a way that we remember our own needs and those of our neighbors in prayer, in suffering, and in loving with Christ. Let us ask him to heal us and his Church and to make us holy. Amen.

ABBREVIATIONS

Frequently Quoted Books
by Joseph Cardinal Ratzinger

CEP   *Church, Ecumenism and Politics: New Essays in Ecclesiology*, trans. Robert Nowell and Dame Frideswide Sandemann, O.S.D. (London: Saint Paul; New York: Crossroad, 1988).

IC   *Introduction to Christianity*, trans. J. R. Foster (Communio Books; San Francisco: Ignatius Press, 2004).

MM   *Milestones: Memoirs 1927–1977*, trans. Erasmo Leiva-Merikakis (San Francisco: Ignatius Press, 1998).

NMT   *The Nature and Mission of Theology: Essays to Orient Theology in Today's Debates*, trans. Adrian Walker (San Francisco: Ignatius Press, 1995).

PCM   *Principles of Christian Morality*, with Heinz Schürmann and Hans Urs von Balthasar, trans. Graham Harrison (San Francisco: Ignatius Press, 1986).

PCT   *Principles of Catholic Theology: Building Stones for a Fundamental Theology*, trans. Sr. Mary Frances McCarthy, S.N.D. (San Francisco: Ignatius Press, 1987).

RR   *The Ratzinger Report: An Exclusive Interview on the State of the Church*, with Vittorio Messori, trans. Salvator Attanasio and Graham Harrison (San Francisco: Ignatius Press, 1985).

SE   *Salt of the Earth: Christianity and the Catholic Church at the End of the Millennium*, an interview with Peter

Seewald, trans. Adrian Walker (San Francisco: Ignatius Press, 1997).

TPE   *A Turning Point for Europe? The Church in the Modern World—Assessment and Forecast*, trans. Brian McNeil, C.R.V. (San Francisco: Ignatius Press, 1994).

TT   *Truth and Tolerance: Christian Belief and World Religions*, trans. Henry Taylor (San Francisco: Ignatius Press, 2004).

WWM   *Wahrheit, Werte, Macht: Prüfsteine der pluralistischen Gesellschaft* (Freiburg im Breisgau: Herder, 1993).

INDEX

Académie des Sciences Morales
   et Politiques (Institut de
   France), 134n34, 176
Adenauer, Konrad, 142, 150–51
Adoukonou, Père Bartholome,
   58n33
Advent, 33–34nn24–25
"Advent quality", 132
Africa, 137 39, 174
Agape, 75–76
Alienation, 68, 81, 131
Allen, John L., Jr., 14, 143,
   162–77
Anamnesis, 122, 125–26, 135,
   136n3
Anglican Church, 93
Anglican-Roman Catholic
   International Commission
   (ARCIC), 95
Anthropology, 45–47
Apostolic succession, 59, 95–97
Aristotle, 39, 64, 135
Armagh, Ireland, Anglican
   Archbishop of, 166
Asceticism, 52
Asia, 157–59, 174
Atheism, 108
Augustine, Saint, 39, 122, 126,
   180, 183
   Ratzinger's study of, 31,
      50–51, 72
Austria, 141

Authority,
   Church, 89–104
   Church teaching authority (*see*
      Magisterium)
   freedom and, 83–88
   secular/political, 89, 93,
      105–11
   two separate authorities,
      105–6, 117
   See also Law; Politics; Power;
      State
Autobiography of Benedict XVI.
   See *Milestones: Memoirs
   1927–1977*

Baader, Franz von, 58n33
Balasuriya, Tissa, 175
Balthasar, Hans Urs von, 33, 42,
   44
Barth, Karl, 26
Basil the Great, Saint, 122
Bavaria, 26, 140–43, 145–46, 166,
   170n11
Beauty, 16
Belgium, 32
Benedict, the name, 157, 160
Benedict XV, Pope, 144, 156
Benedict XVI, Pope (Joseph
   Ratzinger), 11–17, 37, 43,
   154–55
   election of, 11, 14–16, 143,
      145, 154, 156, 158–59